KAWABONGA!

How did kids—like Sigourney Weaver and John Ritter—get to sit in the Peanut Gallery?

Why didn't viewers get to see Howdy himself for the first three episodes?

What did the "D" on Dilly Dally's shirt stand for?

How did Clarabell come to be?

Who was Princess Summerfall Winterspring?

What was the funniest mishap on the set?

What does Kawabonga mean, anyway?

All the answers, and a story that will delight you from beginning to end, are here in Buffalo Bob's funny, intimate, and wonderfully nostalgic memoir . . .

DONNA McCROHAN, who has been watching TV all her life, has been around longer than most people who can make that claim. This is because her father, who worked for Sylvania when television and Donna were in their infancy, had the first TV set on the block. This accounts for Donna's vivid memories of Mr. Tooth Decay, the Invisible Shield, and Eleanor Roosevelt's margarine commercial.

Today a specialist in vintage television, she has frequently guested on TV and radio talk shows, has been a regular contributor to numerous media magazines, and is the author of such books as *The Honeymooners Companion: The Kramdens and the Nortons Revisited*, *The Life and Times of Maxwell Smart*, and *Prime Time Our Time: America's Life and Times Through the Prism of Television*. Her books are well known throughout the media field. Her article, "Yes, Andy, There Is a Mayberry," was reprinted by the *Congressional Record*, and she has spoken at the Smithsonian Institution on the subject of Ralph Kramden and the Images of Labor.

BUFFALO BOB SMITH and Donna McCrohan

HOWDY and ME

Buffalo Bob's Own Story

Ⓟ

A PLUME BOOK

PLUME • Published by the Penguin Group Penguin Books USA Inc., 375 Hudson Street, New York, New York 10014, U.S.A. • Penguin Books Ltd, 27 Wrights Lane, London W8 5TZ, England • Penguin Books Australia Ltd, Ringwood, Victoria, Australia Penguin Books Canada Ltd, 2801 John Street, Markham, Ontario, Canada L3R 1B4 Penguin Books (N.Z.) Ltd,, 182–190 Wairau Road, Auckland 10, New Zealand Penguin Books Ltd, Registered Offices: Harmondsworth, Middlesex, England

First published by Plume, an imprint of New American Library, a division of Penguin Books USA Inc.

First Printing, November, 1990

10 9 8 7 6 5 4 3 2 1

LIBRARY OF CONGRESS CATALOGING IN PUBLICATION DATA:
Smith, Buffalo Bob, 1917–
Howdy and me : Buffalo Bob's own story / Buffalo Bob Smith and Donna McCrohan.
p. cm.
ISBN 0-452-26521-5 : $12.95
1. Howdy Doody Show (Television program) 2. Smith, Buffalo Bob, 1917– . 3. Entertainers—United States—Biography. I. McCrohan, Donna. II. Title.
PN1992.77.H663S65   1990
791.45′72—dc20   90-7344
CIP

To Mil, my devoted wife and best friend, for sharing all those dreams that would never have come true without her encouragement and support; and to my sons, Robin, Ronnie, and Chris, for all their years of service as my trial Peanut Gallery and junior press agents, and for making me so proud every day of my life.

We are indebted to all those whose
memories, insights, efforts, and
thoughtfulness have helped make this
book possible, particularly Lew Anderson, Pady Blackwood, Bob Cough-
lin, Burt Dubrow, Ita Golzman, Eddie
Kean, Jan Kreher-Policastro, John R.
Kraus, Gary Luke, Larry MacDonald,
Denise Marcil, Jeanne Martinet, Jon-
athan Mintzer, Bobbe and Roger
Muir, Nick Nicholson, Herbert C.
Rice, Christopher Schelling, and
David White, and of course, to all
those wonderful people throughout
the years whose talent and hard work
contributed to our show's success.

CONTENTS

Introduction

by DONNA McCROHAN

TV historians have now come to recognize that Buffalo Bob pioneered the technology of television the way D. W. Griffith's *Birth of a Nation* influenced the movies—and is due every bit as much respect. Bob was, as were many figures of early television, an experienced radio personality. If it hadn't been for Howdy Doody, he might have gone the route of his singer/host radio contemporaries, becoming a game-show host, then a late-night talk-show host. But in the midst of the complex identity crises of the nascent industry—are we radios with pictures? little movies? a diversion of the idle rich or a medium for the masses?—Bob happened into the simple role of Pied Piper to the youth of America. Luckily for the youth of America, he made it his business to make them happy.

What brought Howdy Doody to life was the way Bob related to him. What Howdy and Bob brought to life in us were our very first thoughts and hopes and dreams.

As a result, and without exaggeration, Howdy Doody and Buffalo Bob Smith can be described as icons. To people drawn to the shrine, the smallest details about them have significance, up to the number of Howdy's freckles—forty-eight, one for each state in the Union, until another two were added to honor Alaska and Hawaii. To those too young to have followed the Doodyville saga, the appeal is a nearly complete mystery. This is a tough realization for baby boomers, to whom it's already difficult to acknowledge that a whole generation of adults now exists who have not lived through the entire life of TV. It's also sad, as if these later generations, having missed this part of childhood, missed out on having childhoods altogether.

The view, of course, is biased. When we baby boomers talk about Howdy and Bob, we sound the way our parents did remembering Tom Mix, Flash Gordon, and Saturday afternoon movie matinees. There is, however, a difference. As postwar babies, we had the technology to rerun our past, while our parents had only their fading memories of matinees and Flash and Tom. We *could* watch *I Love Lucy* and *The Honeymooners* year in, year out, into the twilight of our lives. Because we could, we did, and insisted on bringing subsequent generations along with us. The shows of our childhood will be on TV forever. Except *Howdy*. It was live, not filmed for rerun. The loss brought out the rebel in us. When we couldn't bring back *The Howdy Doody Show*, we ushered in the wave of nostalgia that in turn paved the way for the Sixties.

Remember the Sixties? In those years between 1960 and 1970 when no Howdy Doody Time graced the airwaves, the decade erupted in protest, race riots, and demonstrations. Is there a correlation? Don't ask diehard boomers. You might get a resounding yes—from a generation now older than our parents had been when Howdy first came to TV.

Okay, we're still biased. Moreover, we've managed to take it for granted that our cultural history is a legacy for the whole world to share—perhaps because we grew up, from earliest infancy, right along with television; and perhaps because there are so many of us that we can impose our manias on the rest of the world. Which brings us back to the unparalleled influence of *The Howdy Doody Show*: Its thirteen years gave Howdy and Bob a lock on the postwar babies, the greatest number of kids at their most impressionable years for the longest time.

Not all Howdy fans are precisely the same age. Some, born during the war years, were old enough to follow every jot and comma of his adventures and remember them clearly to this day. The younger ones don't remember the stories, and probably took a while to make the distinction between Doodyville characters such as Dilly Dally and commercial characters such as Happy Tooth. Nonetheless, they all came under the spell. Under the influence. There's that word again. Influence. Influence to do what?

Let's begin with the obvious. Kids are bright, but they don't know much yet. Someone has to help them accumulate the uneventful but essential things they have to learn. Someone

The Peanut Gallery—with Princess Summerfall Winterspring (Judy Tyler), me, and Clarabell (Nick Nicholson).

must wholeheartedly sugar-coat the necessarily repetitive reinforcement of each lesson. "Be kind to animals." "Go to bed" ("make sure that you get yourself a good night's rest"). "Save your pennies, soon you'll have a nickel." Moms do this. Dads do this. For 2,500-plus half hours between 1947 and 1960, Buffalo Bob did this. He became, in the process, an honorary parent to every child in America (and the highest-paid baby-sitter in history), while Howdy became every kid's best friend. Bob and Howdy influenced baby boomers long before any other influence outside of home had a chance to get at them. Howdy sang:

If you think you use your feet
When you cross the street,
I'll set you wise.
In the daytime or night,
Look around left and right,
And cross the street with your
 eyes.

Arrangement © Edward G. Kean and Robert E. Smith, 1987

INTRODUCTION ————————————————

You may laugh at the simplicity of "Your pal Howdy knows, if you had fifty toes, you'd still cross the street with your eyes." After all, we're sophisticated, and it's anything but. But ultimately, we're smiling with it, realizing that Howdy probably taught us as much if not more about crossing streets as anyone we ever knew. His song undoubtedly even saved a few lives.

In song and story, *The Howdy Doody Show* taught friendship, brotherhood, and doing unto others as you want them to do unto you. When Howdy ran for "President of all the kids in the United States," he spread the message:

Oh, every day you meet a friend,
But do you know how to greet a
* friend?*
If you don't, I'll tell you how.
Just yell, "Howdy Doody!"
And every day you see a pal,
But do you know how to be a pal?
Well, if you don't, I'll tell you
* how.*
Yell, "Howdy Doody!"
Oh, work will be easy and life will
* be breezy.*
You'll find you can sing like the
* birds.*
Your day will be brighter, your
* heart will be lighter,*
If you use those magic words.
Oh, when a buddy shakes your
* hand,*

Be sure as soon as he takes your
* hand,*
You let him know that you under-
* stand,*
And yell, "Howdy Doody!"
Dodododododododeedooh de doody
* Howdy Doody do.*

Arrangement © Edward G. Kean and Robert E. Smith, 1987

The character of Princess Summerfall Winterspring instructed us about nature. Stitched on the princess's costume were a sun for summer, a leaf for fall, a snowman for winter, and a bird for spring. When seasons changed, the princess assumed center stage for a ceremony. It's the spring equinox. And *why* is it called an equinox? Because there are exactly twelve hours between sunup and sundown. It's the first day of summer. *Why? Because today is the longest day of the year.*

Howdy confided to kids about common fears, such as going to the doctor for his "plastic surgery." With his ingenuous, head-bobbing confidences, he forged reassuring bonds that parents could only wish for.

Bob and Howdy also taught us to spell: "How do you spell Wonder Bread? That's right, W-o-n-d-e-r B-r-e-a-d!" But even then, we learned. Wonder Bread, we discovered, built strong bodies by providing the body's essential building blocks, vitamins and minerals. Bob always says, "Howdy zeroed in on products that moms wouldn't object to buying. We encouraged kids to have a substantial breakfast . . . 'and while you're eating, have Kellogg's Rice Krispies.' We encouraged them to brush their teeth after every meal . . . 'and while you're doing it, use Colgate's because it contains Gardol, which fights Mr. Tooth Decay.' "

Buffalo Bob wouldn't accept a sponsor unless he believed in it, then he hyped it with the zeal of a circus ringmaster. Who knows? Maybe his contagious enthusiasm inculcated in us a sense of brand loyalty and trust in the endorser not limited to Buffalo Bob's sponsors, but by extension applicable in the Nineties to James Garner's camera film and Bill Cosby's pudding.

Once we accept the possibility of influence by extension, a handful of seeming improbables approach the realm of the real. We tend to forget how the subtler shapers of history shape it. Surely, 1950 would have become 1990 without anyone's lifting a finger one way or the other. But how many of the indirect, or unintentional, or diffused seeds that Buffalo Bob planted might have taken root without our even recollecting the source?

☞ As baby boomers grew older, did memories of Howdy and Bob instill a longing in us for the happy, carefree childhood days when the biggest problem was whether Mr. Bluster would take the circus from Howdy? Could this have anything to do with a generation that rebelled tooth and nail against ever having to grow up?

☞ How assiduously did baby boomers emulate Howdy Doody, the ultimate role model of a good little kid—who within Doodyville had certain autonomy and power? Did they hone in on his respect for older people and authority figures—if exercised within reason? Don't forget that Howdy knew mean-spirited Mr. Bluster for a corrupt, corrupting old goat, and stood up to him; and that Howdy's alumni exploded into adulthood with an unprecedented opposition to any authority figures they deemed unworthy of support.

☞ What about the plastic surgery? *The Howdy Doody Show* gave kids a series of ongoing stories complete with tension and conflict to inspire attentive curiosity over what will happen next. Did it mold our taste for stories? Whet our appetites for *Dallas* and *Dynasty*, the top-rated series of boomerdom's middle years?

Farfetched analogies? Irrational praise? Not to a born baby boomer.

It's fashionable lately to debunk heroes, but Bob is an odd choice of guys to debunk. Nasty gossip about Buffalo Bob Smith is about as enticing

Ben Grauer swears Howdy Doody in as "President of All the Kids in the United States," January 1949.

as a rumor that Santa Claus abuses his elves and reindeer. Some have asserted that Bob expected too much from his staff and only wanted things done his way. The same has been said about Jackie Gleason and Milton Berle. But all three were virtual inventors in a field that had no rules, before rules were even envisioned. As such, they were responsible for their inventions—responsible to their employees, their employers, and their audiences. Considering their track record, how wrong could they have been? Anyway, it doesn't matter. What matters is that Howdy always saved the circus.

It's been argued that as soon as Buffalo Bob got in on the ground floor of network kidvid, success was a fait accompli, if only because kids had few alternatives. But consider the other performers who tried and failed. NBC's esteemed Ben Grauer, announcer for the NBC Symphony Orchestra and interviewer of heads of state and royalty, once subbed for Bob on *The*

Howdy Doody Show. He emerged from the fray a wiser man: "I wouldn't have believed it until it happened to me, but I was actually afraid of the kids. Those forty little monsters just glared at me from the Peanut Gallery, defying me to make them laugh."

Anyone can take an easy shot, but it's easier in the long run to acknowledge a grateful debt. Fans constantly tell Bob, "We always felt you were a second father. Maybe closer than our real dads, because you spoke to us every day. By the time our dads got home, we were in bed," and "You were a pal. When you spoke to us on *The Howdy Doody Show*, my sister and I thought you were doing the whole show just for us."

The fact is that Buffalo Bob had and has a rare gift for liking kids so much that he wouldn't know how to patronize them. Says he, "Kids know whether or not you like them. They know when you're nervous, when you can't wait to be rid of them. You can't kid a kid."

So a whole generation of kids listened to Buffalo Bob. When he prefaced a bit of friendly advice with "And you know, kids," you knew, kids. You knew he spoke from his heart to your heart. You made a major effort to do what he asked you to do.

When he said it on the Thanksgiving 1987 fortieth anniversary special, parents reacted with a flash of recognition long forgotten. Kids reacted as kids always do to Buffalo Bob, with rapt attention. And the next day, kids at school could talk about nothing but Doodyville.

We as a generation, probably as a nation, are indebted to Howdy Doody and Buffalo Bob. For a long, long time, they made that impression on all of us.

Kawabonga.

THE BUFF MEETS THE BOOMER

When my co-author, Donna McCrohan, was introduced to me, she was described as a "professional baby boomer." I told her I'm not very fond of the phrase *baby boomers*. I just don't like the sound of it. I hate the word *yuppies*. I prefer *alumni*, and I consider Howdy's and my alumni to be *all* the kids who sat in the actual Peanut Gallery and *also* in the extended Peanut Gallery, in homes across America from sea to shining sea. Then I asked her what a professional baby boomer did, and she said she wrote books about classic TV shows. I suggested that maybe this made her a TV critic, and she assured me that she wasn't critical enough to be a critic; she only writes about shows she cares about, and her inclination is to praise them to the skies. I figured this made her a good choice to work with me on this book.

I wondered when she first saw Howdy and me, and she said, "I think I remember being very little, barely old enough to talk, and the folks came home with a TV set. They showed me how to work it, and I sent them away until dinner. Once *Howdy* came on, the only way I ever ate dinner was in front of the TV set." Then she continued, "Buffalo Bob, shouldn't I be asking you the questions?" So she did, and you'll find excerpts of our conversations peppered throughout this book.

I hope you enjoy reading *Howdy and Me* as much as we enjoyed putting it together. It enabled me to relive the happiest times of my life—so many of which were happy because I shared them with you.

Buffalo B B Smith

1

I COULD HAVE BEEN
STAUNTON STAN

One day I was called out of rehearsal. Our director told me that Niles Trammell, president of NBC, wanted to talk to me on the telephone. I went to the phone in the control room and he asked, "Hey, Bob, what kind of show have you got there, that *Howdy Doody*?" In response, I asked him to clarify his question. He elaborated, "I've never needed a ticket for anything. What's going on?"

He then told me he had to get a boy into the show that night but couldn't scare up a ticket: "His father is going to bring him to my office and is going to watch the show with me up here, and his grandfather is going to watch the show at home. But I'm told he can't get into the show without a ticket. What am I going to do? Lots of people are going to be disappointed."

"Blame the fire laws. There's a very strict ceiling on the number of kids we can admit to the Peanut Gallery, and there's a fireman on duty to be sure we observe it."

After I explained the fireman's no-sneak rule, I had an inspiration: "We'll be doing a Welch's Grape Juice commercial. I'm going to be drinking grape juice and offer some to a kid seated next to me in the gallery. I think I can take the boy into the studio with me if I tell the fireman that he's appearing in a commercial, because then he will technically be a model, an actor, not just another kid in the Peanut Gallery. If you guarantee me that

From: **NILES TRAMMELL**

Date February 1 1950

To: Mr Bob Smith

Please

	File.		Return to me with your comments or recommendations.
	For your information.		
	For suitable action.		Route to interested persons in your organization.
	Note and return.		
	Phone me.		See me.
	Reply direct.		
	Retain papers.		

Remarks:

The attached note from the Honorable Herbert Hoover's grandchild is a note that you might like to keep.

Niles Trammell

EXEC. 1-(2-47)

Mementos of Andrew Hoover's visit to the Peanut Gallery.

TELETYPE NY 1-1333 / TELEPHONE: ELDORADO 5-3000

The WALDORF-ASTORIA

PARK AND LEXINGTON AVENUES / 49TH AND 50TH STREETS / NEW YORK 22

Dear Mr. Trammel
Thankyou for leting me come
to the Howdy Doody show
I liked it very much.
Love
from
andrew
Hoover

FOR AIR MAIL OR FOREIGN MAIL USE

he'll like Welch's Grape Juice, I'll do this."

"I guarantee he'll like Welch's Grape Juice."

"Fine. Have your secretary bring him to my office at five-fifteen."

"Don't you want to know his name?"

"What is it?"

"Andrew Hoover. President Herbert Hoover's grandson."

Thank God Andrew liked Welch's Grape Juice. But I'm not exaggerating the difficulty of getting him into the show. In the Fifties, pregnant women would write way in advance for tickets for their unborn children. It didn't help. You had to have inside connections to get into the gallery. What I've since realized is that these same inside connections led to entry-level jobs in TV.

Some worrywart once wrote that our Peanuts were disillusioned by being herded down corridors, by Bob Keeshan policing them into order, by the studio lights, and by the unglamorous real-life stage. The truth, however, is that the experience didn't come as a total shock to these children with parents and relatives in television. More likely the experience, combined with their parents' or relatives' connections, heightened their interest in the medium.

Perhaps some little tykes couldn't handle the adventure. (Some little tykes bawl hysterically when they can't find their toes.) Yet I can't help reflecting, with tremendous pride, that a disproportionate number of executives currently starring in and running the media sat in our studio in the Peanut Gallery.

Peanut Gallery regular Sigourney Weaver, the daughter of NBC president Pat Weaver, comes instantly to mind. So does John Ritter, son of singing cowboy Tex Ritter. Bart Andrews, who had no NBC connections as a child, waited four years for tickets, writing for them almost every week, until a cousin joined NBC as a secretary. Two days later he had tickets. Today Bart's a TV comedy writer and the author of upward of a dozen books about television. Eileen Bradley had a long wait too, until someone who worked for NBC moved into the neighborhood. Then she got tickets. Today Eileen books guests on *The Pat Sajak Show*. And Carl Bernstein of the history-making journalistic team of Woodward and Bernstein once won a Howdy Doody look-alike contest.

The list could go on and on, but I'm getting ahead of myself. By the time Doodyville had its Peanut Gallery, I was almost as old as our alumni are now. This naturally raises the question of what I managed to do with my life in the thirty years before Howdy walked into it. A confirmed fan of unstinting diligence and effort, I'm happy to say I was anything but idle. I'd go so far as to call myself a workaholic except that I have to confess, I

My wonderful parents in their wedding portrait, taken May 1903.

play at least as hard as I work. I believe in fun and hope I was able to impart a good deal of it—and above all, an abiding respect for it—to the generation of children who grew up watching Howdy and me on TV.

In a nutshell, "Buffalo Bob" isn't a stage name. I was born Buffalo Bob. My parents named me Robert, and I was born in Buffalo, New York, so the name *Buffalo* even appears on my birth certificate, along with the date: November 27, 1917. The family name

that appears there is Schmidt, not Smith, but even the Smith part isn't entirely a concession to the stage. When I was eighteen, working in radio, and receiving paychecks as Robert Schmidt, one of the writers built a few Personal Finance commercials around me as Smilin' Bob Smith. After that, I'd get some checks made out to Schmidt and others to Smith, and my banker said it didn't seem overwhelmingly kosher for me to be cashing checks made out to two different people. I agreed in theory but put off the paperwork until two weeks before I married my wife, then legally changed my name to Smith to relieve her of having to change her name twice.

At the time I had every intention of staying in radio. The idea of being on television seemed as far off as the moon—which, in 1940, seemed a whole lot farther off than it does today, a half century later. When I married Mil, I was still years away from working with children on radio, years away from talking to myself while pretending that my second voice belonged to a character named Elmer, and nearly a decade away from giving Elmer a body and a new name, the name Howdy Doody.

And now, let's go back to the beginning.

My maternal grandfather, Gotthold Kuehn (pronounced "Grandpa Keen"), was a Lutheran minister in

Staunton, Illinois. He and Grandma Kuehn had ten children. My mother, Emma, as their oldest, was expected to help raise the family. She therefore didn't get as much of an education as she otherwise might have. But school did provide her with the opportunity to know my father, Emil H. Schmidt. Mom and Dad were in the first grade together, went to school together, and were confirmed together. Then they married. Grandpa Kuehn officiated at the ceremony. Then they had three children: Elvin, in 1905; Esther, in 1906; and Victor, 1908.

My dad worked as a miner in Staunton, in Mine Number One, where they mined soft coal. One day the whistle sounded. Whenever the whistle blew, the entire town held its breath. How bad was the accident? Who wouldn't come out alive? The women would run down the streets in their aprons, praying that their husbands, sons, brothers, and sweethearts had survived.

On this particular day, my father was one of three men to step out uninjured. Hundreds died. My mother said to him, "Emil, that's the last day you're going down into that mine." And it was.

They had relatives in the Buffalo area and other relations around Indianapolis. They flipped a coin—for all I know, it might have been a Buffalo nickel—and Buffalo won. If it had been Indianapolis, I might have been Indianapolis Irving. If they'd never moved, I might have been Staunton Stan Smith. As things transpired, I must have been conceived in Staunton, because Mom and Dad had me only a few months after they'd transplanted the family to New York.

I grew up close to my family. My sister Esther and I were the best of buddies. Other little girls had dolls, but she had me. She'd push me around in her carriage, or let her friends take turns pushing it, for what seems to have been the first ten years of my life. By my second decade, I'd moved up to double dating with her fairly often.

One of my earliest childhood memories is of being toilet trained, because that was the only way we got Necco wafers. If we did our business in the right place, it earned us a Necco. When mother shopped for Neccos, she never asked for them by name but always as "pot wafers." The grocery clerk always knew what she meant.

One afternoon I went over to my cousin Ray's. Ray was a day older than I, and we were both "in training." When Uncle Chris took me home, Mother asked, "Robert, what did you and Cousin Ray do this afternoon?" I greeted her with a jubilant "Edna tanny Ray poop." Mother said, "What's that, Robert?" I blurted again, "Edna tanny Ray poop." Mystified, mother phoned Aunt Edna, who explained that Ray hadn't done his business in the potty, but I had performed properly and had gotten candy. In other words, Edna gave me

These are my confirmation pictures—Emmaus Lutheran Church, Buffalo, New York—taken on Palm Sunday, 1930.

candy, but Ray lost out because he misdirected his poop.

When Mil and I toilet trained our three children, we used the phrase, combined of course with the wafers. It has also surfaced through the decades whenever we asked our children, "So, what's doing?" They've been likely as not to answer "Oh, Edna tanny Ray poop."

Another early memory is of Buster, our family canary. He sang like a charm. But one morning we woke up to discover that Buster had chirped his last note. He lay on the floor of the cage, dead. At three and absolutely devastated, I cried as if my heart would burst. I couldn't believe Buster was gone. My parents couldn't console me. My dad got a cigar box, and Mother decorated it with fancy fabric to make a lovely coffin. We took the coffin to Dad's favorite rose garden, dug a hole, held a ceremony, put Buster in the ground, and set a headstone over him. My parents, much relieved, noticed I took it very well, and I seemed to be feeling better.

But after that, my first priority each morning was to rush out to the rose garden, dig up the dirt, open the cigar box, and examine Buster to see if he had resurrected yet. Shucks. No luck. Still dead. Okay, better luck next time. Back into the box he'd go. I'd bury him again, replacing his headstone. Then I'd wake up the next morning, race to the roses, and repeat the process. Dig him up. Stare at him. Shake him. Nothing. Put him back. Again. And again. Until Mother spotted me and issued an emphatic "Robert, don't dig up that canary."

This, too, has become a by-word in our family. Whenever someone dredges up the past, or tries to haul out skeletons best left in the closet, we silence the griper with an uncompromising "Oh, for pity's sake, don't dig up the canary."

Throughout my childhood, I had a habit of fainting. Apparently my stomach distended if something excited me, rising into my rib cage and pressing against my heart. In grammar school I lost a spelling bee thanks to this condition. We'd gone into the final rounds, with only little Mildred Metz and me still standing. Pressure got the better of me. Instead of spelling my word, I keeled over. The teacher and principal revived me, but Mildred won the bee.

My father had musical ability. He'd played trombone in the Staunton band. But Grandpa Kuehn, the minister, had strict views on bands and dances. He didn't approve, putting them in the same category as playing cards: "Too wordly for a good Christian." He made Dad promise to give up bands and band concerts. As much as Dad loved the trombone, he gave in, because he knew that if he didn't, Mom would have been forbidden to marry him.

Though Grandpa Kuehn considered band instruments to be tawdry and reprehensible, he had no objections to my mother's learning piano. Maybe what she absorbed rubbed off on me. I couldn't have been much more than eight when we discovered that I could play practically any tune on the keyboard simply by hearing it. Whether "Jingle Bells" or a church hymn, I picked it out as soon as I sat down, without having to fish for any notes. My mother supplemented this by teaching me what she knew, and then Dad decided on more formal training. He took me to Clara Mueller, a very fine Eastman School of Music–trained pianist, church organist, and piano teacher. Dad made me practice an hour a day. On days when he didn't work, he sat with me to enforce the edict. When he did work, the first question from his lips when he came home was invariably "Did Bob practice?" I couldn't go out to play until I'd done my hour.

One day Dad came home and mother confessed that I hadn't done my hour yet because my football team needed me for a play-off, but I'd practice the minute I got home. Dad said, "No, I want him to practice *before* he goes out to play." When I came through the door, Dad confronted me with "You didn't practice."

I said, "I will now."

He reached toward me. "Give me your football." I gave it to him, and he took me down to the cellar, where he grabbed a butcher knife, plunged it into the ball, knocked the air out of the ball, threw it into the furnace, and made me watch it burn. This he followed with a jovial "Now, when do we practice?"

"I guess before I play football."

Did destiny decree that I'd be forever inseparable from the piano? Heck, no. Dad did that.

I learned quickly, studied the classics, and acquired something of a reputation as a prodigious child. At age eleven, after giving me no more than six organ lessons, Clara contracted pneumonia and couldn't play at Sunday services. Her father, Emil Mueller, the Lutheran minister, called my dad, also an Emil, and asked if he would bring me to church: "Clara's very ill and we can't get an organist. I'm sure Robert can play the service. Please come over with him, and we'll find out." They decided I was ready. Fortunately, my dad stood next to me during the service, and thanks to his support and Clara's lessons, I played without a hitch. When Clara recovered, we resumed lessons as usual, though I'd already turned semipro.

By the end of that year I worked as an accompanist at the Emblem Theatre when they had amateur nights, and played the organ before the evening newsreels. The Emblem paid me in free passes. I could go as often as I pleased and bring all the guests I cared to. On dish night, when everyone got a free dish just for paying admission, I'd get several dishes. When Cy's Country Store sponsored grocery-night raffles, a most mysterious quirk of fate arranged that my mom or I would always be holding one of the lucky numbers.

My father and in fact my whole family, and the whole country, were in awe of radio. I think people conjured up pictures while listening to their sets—Amos 'n' Andy's Fresh Air taxicab, Jack Benny's Maxwell, Fibber McGee and Molly's closet. Molly warned, "Fibber, don't open that closet!" Always too late. Then came the sound effects, tumbling, crashing, banging. We could visualize every single object that landed on Fibber's head. Every Sunday night everybody would flock around the radio to hear Jack Benny. Benny and Fred Allen had their feud going then, contrived of course, but effective. We couldn't wait to devour what Benny was going to say next about Allen and, at a later hour, how Allen was going to verbally barbecue Benny.

And *The Shadow.* When my dad listened to the Shadow, we didn't dare distract him. And the heavyweight championships. And Franklin Delano Roosevelt's *Fireside Chats.* Sometimes we'd have house parties. My dad would send me to the bakery to get fresh rolls, and we'd get ham and cheese for sandwiches, and that would be a big night. Ten or twelve people around the radio, adults and children. I'm indebted to television, but I just don't see where television ever, ever had this impact, this total ability to absorb the imagination of everyone in the room.

There used to be a radio program on WGR in the Buffalo area called *The Boys Club of the Air.* One night they'd have a spelling bee. Another evening might feature a string trio. Always starring children ranging in age from maybe ten to fifteen years old. My father and I would listen to it, and before long, we couldn't just listen. No, he urged and encouraged me to audition for it. I finally went to a man named Herbert C. Rice, who produced and directed the show. I'd say he hired me right away, but if "hired" implies

"paid," then nobody hired me. He did, however, bring me aboard to play piano in the orchestra, sing in the boy choristers, perform with an instrumental string trio, and, when we had spelling bees, announce the words the contestants had to spell.

I began with *Boys Club* at age eleven and stayed with them for a year, when they went off the air. By then I'd faithfully put in two, three, and four nights each week, gaining the sort of experience I could never have bought at any price.

In 1933, my last year in high school, I became friendly with two other boys, Johnny Eisenberger and Elmer Hattenberger, when we appeared in a Gilbert and Sullivan operetta. Johnny, with his exceptional baritone voice, had been runner-up in the prestigious New York State Atwater Kent auditions. The three of us formed a vocal trio. I arranged for an audition with Herb Rice at WGR. He liked us enough to send us home to practice, practice, practice, get ourselves a repertoire, and come back when we felt really ready. Maybe WGR would find a place for us.

You may remember 1933 as the year of repeal of Prohibition. Yes, indeed. So one of the biggest breweries in Buffalo, Simon Brewery, promoted itself with its own radio show, *Simon Supper Club of the Air.* (Does an impression emerge of radio as a series of "clubs of the air"? We saw it just that way. Informal, involving, and

The Hi-Hatters Trio. I was 15.

with an ingratiating intimacy that TV, for the most part, isn't geared to achieve.)

Simon Supper Club ran from 7:00 to 7:30 P.M. Monday, Wednesday, and Friday on WBEN, the station owned by *The Buffalo Evening News.* Our trio, practiced, repertoired, and champing at the bit, jumped at the chance to audition when Simon Brewery advertised for new acts. Because Hattenberger, Eisenberger, and Schmidt wasn't euphonious enough, we became the Hi-Hatters. And were hired. For money. Twenty-five dollars a show—huge money during the

Depression—for three shows a week. This enabled us to pocket $25 *each* per week. I could have dropped through the floorboards with joy.

This happened August 23, 1933. I'll never forget the date. Elated, I walked from downtown Buffalo to my home, at least three miles away on Roehrer Avenue. I couldn't stop grinning and whistling, and nearly splitting in two to tell my father, mother, brothers, and sister the good news. When I at last reached the top of the stairs in our house, at about six o'clock at night, my mother was standing there.

"Robert, go to Dr. Ellison right away. Tell him to come over. And hurry. Your daddy is very sick."

I ran to the doctor's, catching him in the middle of his meal. He put down his fork and drove me home immediately, but when we arrived, my father was already dead. Dead of a heart attack at fifty years old, without ever having learned that I had my first paying radio job.

Dad had worked so hard. First in the mines. Then he did carpentry work at Fort Porter, a World War I army base in Buffalo. When that dried up at the end of the war, he did carpentry for independent contractors. On one job, as men poured concrete several floors above him, a wet slab hit my father in the eye. He wiped his eye and went back to work. There's lime in concrete, and the pain must have been intense, but he finished the day. Someone said, "Emil, your eye is all bloodshot." He stopped by a doctor's office on the way home. Instead of irrigating the eye with cold water, the doctor put drops in it and bandaged it. The bandage came off the next morning, and my father never saw from that eye again.

Considering the hardship Dad endured, I'd have loved to give him the joy of sharing in my success. If he'd lived another hour, or if I'd auditioned a few hours earlier, he could have had a taste of what was to come. He didn't, but fortunately my mother lived long enough to revel in every minute. Even to appear on *The Howdy Doody Show*. More on that later.

Simon Supper Club ran for something like twenty-six weeks. When it ran its course, we went back to Herb Rice, who hired us to appear on both stations of the Buffalo Broadcasting Corporation (BBC)—WGR and WKBW. Then Kate Smith came to town.

Kate's show on CBS had a tremendous following. Within the next few years she'd so completely impressed the network that she had one of the two noncancelable contracts in radio—the other one going to Jack Benny—meaning only war could force her off the air. *The Kate Smith Show*, sponsored by the Hudson Motor Car Company (Hudson Terraplane Automobile), went on to distinguish itself as one of the top-rated shows on radio for two decades.

The Hi-Hatters and another 950 acts tried out when Kate came to Buffalo. We won, along with a very talented gal soprano, and were whisked to New York City. We earned perhaps $200 each plus first-class train fare and a week at the St. Moritz Hotel, all expenses paid.

Tom Kennedy, the "Voice of RKO," heard us there and introduced us to his wife, Mickey Feeley. He put the four of us together with a writer who came up with special lyrics and material. I did the musical arrangements. Mickey sang, danced, and did a cute Betty Boop number wearing a Betty Boop head over her own. As a foursome, we played vaudeville in and

Johnny Eisenberger of Jack and Gil (right), Foster Brooks (center), and I (left) in a gag shot for Bell Aircraft.

around New York for three or four months—Coney Island and Brooklyn, Staten Island, the Bronx, and Queens. We lived for the duration in the Hotel Chesterfield on 49th Street. I can't call it a fleabag, but it depressed us. It certainly wasn't home.

What can I say? We got homesick. At the ripe old age of sixteen or seventeen, I wanted to be with my family again. Johnny, about four years older than I, felt the same. Elmer, at twenty-one or twenty-two, developed an interest in what looked to us like wild living. Not liking the big city any more, I called Herb Rice.

Herb delighted me with his re-sponse: "Robert, you come back. I've got a surprise for you." Johnny and I returned to Buffalo. WGR, a CBS affiliate, had two staff pianists. One was leaving to get married. Herb gave me her job. Johnny Eisenberger and I formed a duo, Jack and Gil. Herb put us on three or four times a week, doing a fifteen-minute feed to the Columbia Broadcasting System.

It was the height of the Depression. My friend Cliff Jones and I got interested in launching a summer theater, partly because the Alhambra night club on the shores of Lake Erie could be rented at a bargain-basement rate. We paid a few hundred dollars to have it for the whole summer, rented chairs, built little tables, and sold beer in addition to tickets to the show. We called it The Roadside Theater. My mother, convinced it meant Roadhouse, worried that I might be running a dive.

One night, en route to the Roadside, I saw Mil Metz across the street. I'd gone through grammar school, P.S. 53, with little Mildred Metz of spelling bee fame. A smart gal, she had won the Jesse Ketchum Medal for the most scholastically outstanding student in western New York. (I was runner-up.) We used to ice skate together at the Humboldt Park Skating Rink, checking our shoes for a nickel before we skated. Then the street I lived on separated our high school districts, so she went to East High School and I to Masten Park (later Fosdick-Masten) High. We dated on and off, but not very often until that night. I asked her to be my guest at our summer theater.

That's when we became, in the jargon of the era, "an item"—and I'll tell you right now that she much prefers being called Mil, rather than Mildred or even Millie. I put Mil to work at the Roadside right away. I sold tickets, while she collected them at the door. We went to the theater every night, staying until the show had opened and we'd counted the money. The theater closed that autumn, but Mil and I continued dating. Frequently I'd plan to take her to the movies, but Herb Rice would surprise me with a musical arrangement or other assignment that had to be ready by the next morning. Instead of seeing a movie, I'd be at the piano in my mother's living room. Mil would sit in the chair next to me. We smoked like chimneys, drank beer, and worked until eleven or eleven-thirty. I'd take Mil home, then head back to the piano to finish the music.

Presumably because we thrive on the same kind of punishment, Mil and I couldn't get around the fact that we were in love. Miserable timing. Out of the Depression and into World War II. But life will do that to you. I knew poverty; my family had never had much money. Mil knew it too, for entirely opposite reasons. Her father, Gustav Adolph Metz, the second oldest of ten children, had arrived in the United States without a dime. He got a job in a grocery store, then owned the grocery store, then became a contractor, eventually building Buffalo's City Hall, several landmark theaters, and a significant hunk of Cornell University. A selfmade multimillionaire in the 1920s, he lost every cent in the 1929 crash. To avoid bankruptcy, he sold his earthly possessions and cashed in his life insurance to settle with his creditors—ending up as strapped for funds as the rest of us.

But what about Mil and me? You're young and hopelessly sold on living out your life with one person and one person only, the person sitting beside your piano, smoking, drinking beer, caring about your work. What do you do? In the summer of 1940, moping in a restaurant after a date, Mil and I took out a pencil and the back of an envelope to calculate how far we could go on the $60 a week I earned. She made $14 a week, but I wanted to be able to support her myself.

It was Weiss's Restaurant, where the world's most exquisite ham and cheese sandwiches on rye sold for 15 cents each and draft beer went for a dime. We didn't have much money, but we had as much as anybody had. Her father would build an apartment for us over her parents' house. As we shook our heads, uncertain as to whether we could get by, the jukebox played "I'll Get By (As Long As I

Have You)." We instantly made it our song and our sign to take the plunge. Even today when I play the song, Mil runs over, gives me a kiss, and we think about incredibly tasty ham and cheese sandwiches.

We tied the knot on Thanksgiving Day, 1940. That morning I did two radio broadcasts, then played a church service. The ceremony took place at 5:00 P.M., leaving a big three and a half days for our honeymoon in Cleveland and Buffalo before I had to be back to work.

Many years later, when Edward R. Murrow had us as guests on his *Person to Person* show, he asked Mil when she first realized we might be serious. She said it was in the fourth grade, because I'd written the following verse in her autograph book:

Roses are red.
Violets are blue.
Garlic is strong,
And I'm garlic for you.

Young love is certainly amazing. Who but a very small child—or maybe Count Dracula—would equate passion with garlic?

Anyway, Mil contends to this day that I married her to keep the Jesse Ketchum Medal in the family.

Times improved professionally. Herb gave me a whole show. I sang, played the piano, and teamed with Buffalo's finest gal vocalist, Elvera

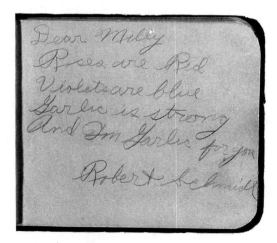

Here's the poem. Mil saved her autograph book!

Ruppel. On this program, *Bob and Vera*, I really started to branch out.

I still see Herb, who says I was a driven man in those days: "Bob drove himself harder than anyone I've ever known. I'd load him down with work and even though he'd protest 'You're killing me,' he'd do it. After arranging the score, he'd have to copy all the individual parts for each of the eighteen or twenty musicians and then make vocal arrangements for each of the singers.

"Bob could be tough on himself and equally tough on others. He never actually took time off to relax, so he'd unwind by kidding around. One of the women he sang with had a bottom that wobbled like jelly. Bob used to tease her by wobbling it."

This shot of Mill and me was taken in 1946 at the home of Herb Rice.

My hard work paid dividends in the form of my first big money in radio. In 1942 Herb Rice called me into his office. The BBD&O advertising agency (Batten, Barton, Durstine, & Osborn Inc., known locally as Cotton Battin' Worsted and Iodine), also in our building, represented the Corning Glassworks. Herb told me, "BBD&O wants to broadcast a talent show, and all the talent will be selected from the Corning Glassworks in Corning, New York." Corning took its community relations seriously. They'd built a big memorial clubhouse with bowling alleys and pool tables. Now they wanted to do more. They needed somebody who could write it, produce it, emcee it, audition the acts, direct the band and the glee club, and do musical arrangements.

I met with the Corning people and understood immediately what they had in mind. A similar show, *The Wheeling Steelmakers*, originated from Wheeling, West Virginia. I'd been making between $50 and $60 a week, and killing myself to make that kind of money. Besides doing my radio shows, I'd do country clubs on Saturday nights with five or six of Buffalo's top musicians. Now Corning offered me $250 for a weekend's labor. I'd take the 6:00 P.M. train from Buffalo on Friday, arriving in Corning at 9:30. I'd rehearse the glee club that evening until midnight, then all day Saturday rehearse the other acts and audition new talent. Sometimes we

featured local high school bands. We broadcast the program on WENY Elmira and WHCU Ithaca on Sunday afternoon from the Masonic Cathedral, the largest auditorium in Corning. And I'd be back home by Sunday night, ready to discharge my Monday-through-Friday assignments on WGR and WKBW.

For many years WGR had on its roster the top-rated morning man in Buffalo, Clint Buehlman. Clint virtually cornered the ratings. Clint and his wife Evelyn, and Mil and I, became great friends. WBEN, the city's biggest and best station, lured Clint away to do their morning show. I stayed on with WGR.

Like cities across the nation during the war years, Buffalo held bond rallies on a regular basis. We held ours during lunch hour, noon to one, in Lafayette Square off Main Street. Every day a different Buffalo personality would host the hour, introduce the entertainment, and generally sell significant numbers of bonds and stamps. Clint Buehlman did it one day, Foster Brooks another, and on the afternoon that I did it, rain forced us to set up indoors, on the mezzanine floor of the William Hengerer Department Store. "Wee" Bonnie Baker, in town to play Harry Altman's Williamsville Glen, joined me for the occasion. Her re-

Left to right: Johnny Eisenberger, Foster Brooks, Buffalo announcer John Boothby, and I, about to do a show for Bell Aircraft during World War II.

cording of "Oh, Johnny, Oh, Johnny, Oh!" was sweeping the country at the time, making her very popular, very hot.

I met with her just before the rally, in the office of Julian Trivers, head of promotion, advertising, and public relations for Hengerer's. I don't think mornings agreed with Bonnie. After all, her night club appearances at Altman's kept her up late. She had dark glasses on and looked like she'd pay a small fortune to beg off and be back home, asleep. I bent over backward to be cordial.

"Bonnie, I hope you're going to sing 'Oh, Johnny' for us today."

"Are you kidding? I can't even spit before eleven o'clock."

I bet her that we could sell $5,000 worth of bonds if she'd sing her song. She didn't want to sing without a band. I told her that I played her records all the time, knew the song, knew her arrangement and key, and could accompany her on the piano. She didn't believe me until I did it for her on the spot. Then she caved in, did a fantastic job for the rally, sang her solo, warbled a few more with me, and we made

good on my bet. I don't remember the exact figure, but I do know we broke some kind of record for previous bond and stamp sales.

> DONNA: Which do you prefer, TV or radio?
> BOB: Radio. It's more relaxed. I'd be on the air two and a half hours in the morning and I'd feel like I was talking to just you or just her or just him. To me, there's nothing relaxing about television. You feel you're on the spot every minute. Driving, smashing, working in a barn.

The mid-Forties found me doing *Stump Bob Smith* with Foster Brooks from Grant's Department Store on Main Street, Buffalo.

If you've ever seen Johnny Carson's "Stump the Band" segment, you've already got the picture. People sent us song titles on postcards. If members of the audience had heard of the song, I had to play it. If I couldn't, the person who stumped me would win a war stamp. War stamps were stamps purchased as downpayments of sorts on Series E War Bonds. When a person's $1, $2, and $5 war stamps and cash added up to $18.75, the stamps could be traded in for a Series E bond worth $25 at maturity ten years later. We awarded each stumper a $1 war stamp for stumping Bob Smith. For the same feat, Johnny Carson gives dinner for two. Don't blame me. It's inflation.

Herb Rice devised an idea for a new show, *The Cheer Up Gang*. I emceed it, produced it, directed the band, and wrote the comedy scripts and most of the vocal arrangements. On *The Cheer Up Gang* we'd entertain people in hospitals, nursing homes, and the like. He sold Mutual Broadcasting Company on doing it every morning, 11:00 to 11:30 A.M., on the full Mutual Radio Network. We had a sixteen-piece band and a vocal foursome known as the Four Cheers. The Four Cheers consisted of Charlie Parlato, Nick Nicholson, Elvera, and me. Charlie, who sang and played the trumpet, later went with Lawrence Welk. Nick, who sang and played trombone, had gone all through high school with my wife, Mil. When I was fifteen, Nick and I dated twins. I admired Nick's talent and liked him as a friend, so it shouldn't be too surprising that I brought him to New York in later years to *The Howdy Doody Show*.

The Four Cheers sang straight and also silly. We did a take-off on the Ink Spots, called the Pink Spots, that can best be described as awfully broad humor. A lot of what we did on *The Cheer Up Gang* might seem hokey by today's standards, but everyone had terrific fun with it then. I can honestly say that we delivered solid, high-spirited entertainment.

At about this time, my brother Vic and I entered the ski-ball business. Vic had been a cigar salesman, a Dutch

Masters representative, professionally intimate with every good saloon in Buffalo, Lackawana, Tonawanda, Niagara Falls, and points north, south, east, and west. I was entertaining at clubs and house parties when not on the air. At one party I met Homer Capehart, who later became the Republican Senator Capehart from Indiana. But then he resided in our area, where he'd helped save the Wurlitzer Organ Company. Wurlitzer had faced financial death when people stopped buying pipe organs. Mr. Capehart persuaded Wurlitzer to put its technology into jukeboxes and nickelodeons. Then they developed the ski-ball machine, which had a long alley, wooden balls, and a series of holes with point values. I first played ski-ball at this party, and accosted the future senator. "Hey! Wouldn't these do great in saloons?" He told me that's what they were made for. Not many private homes had them. They were designed for bars. But they had no distribution.

Vic and I had wanted to go into some project together anyhow. I proposed this to Vic and set a date with Homer. Wurlitzer sold us three machines at $259.50 apiece—$100 down and $15.95 for ten weeks thereafter. We placed them in spots that Vic selected. They took off. Buffalo went wild over ski-ball. We built up our fleet to over fifty machines. I continued with my radio shows and outside entertaining, and raced around upstate New York repairing ski-ball games at night.

Eventually I told Vic, "This is no fun. You do it. It's yours, the whole ski-ball empire." He wanted to pay me. I refused cash. He said, "Will you let me buy your automobiles for the next four or five years?" That made sense. I got cars. He got the ski-ball business. I concentrated on show biz.

In the spring of 1943 Julian Trivers, who'd watched me cajole Bonnie in his office and sell all those bonds from Hengerer's mezzanine, came up with an idea for an audience-participation show starring the biggest name in town—Clint Buehlman—and his buddy from WGR, Bob Smith. Because Herb Rice left WGR to go to New York to become writer–producer for Gabriel Heatter's extremely high-rated newscast on the Mutual Network, I had lost my loyalty to WGR and happily returned to WBEN, the station that had given me my very first paid radio job.

WBEN had Clint on from 6:00 to 9:00 A.M., pulling in fine ratings. The news, 9:00 to 9:15, kept up the ratings. But then the ratings would fall apart, because the whole world next listened to Don MacNeil's *Breakfast Club* from Chicago. As a matter of fact, CBS and NBC didn't start feeding the network affiliates until 10:00 in the morning Eastern time, because there didn't seem to be much point. So Don had the only network show on at 9:00 A.M.

and had a firm grip on the ratings for every city in the United States. Local stations thought twice before pitting anything against him, considering it a likely waste of money.

Julian Trivers had enough faith in Buehlman and Smith to team us for the 9:15 to 10:00 *Early Date At Hengerer's*. He hired me to sing, play the piano, co-emcee, write the show, and produce it. We did stunts with the audience, for instance awarding a prize to the lady with the heaviest handbag—provided that she allowed us to go through the handbag to describe what it contained. We had ladies compete to see who could scream the longest without taking a breath. A dozen long-stemmed roses went to the oldest grandmother, or the woman who had come the farthest, or the mom with the most children. We'd have the volunteer fire department as guests, or the wives of the volunteer fire department, or the sewing circle from Emmaus Lutheran Church on Southampton Street. We played "Stump Bob Smith." As I recall, we had a rating of maybe three when we launched this—while Don MacNeil had a seventeen or so. After six months, our homey, friendly, unpretentious local *Early Date At Hengerer's* outranked Don MacNeil in our region better than three to one.

After a year of tremendous success on *Early Date*, WBEN persuaded me to resign from the Corning job. I said, "Gee, guys, that's good money

you want me to give up." So they offered me better than double the money, plus my own 12:30 to 1:30 show (in addition to *Early Date*), plus the Sunday afternoon *Quiz of Two Cities* on which rival cities, like Rochester and Buffalo, competed for mighty modest riches and acclaim. I'd ask the questions of the Buffalo contingent, then an emcee in the other town would ask the same questions of our competitors. We did these live, and local audiences would be totally enthralled.

By 1946 I was making over $600 a week in local Buffalo radio.

Bob Thompson, WBEN's general manager, suggested that the NBC network look more closely at *Early Date* with the possibility of originating it from Buffalo for the network, or perhaps of bringing it to New York City. NBC concluded that we could attribute its success to the way we harnessed local flavor, local topics, local appeal—and therefore convinced itself that whatever we did right would be wrong for network fare. But for several years they had been looking for a personality to do their early-morning radio show on WEAF (later WNBC), the flagship station of the National Broadcasting Company for the New York metropolitan area.

In those years Arthur Godfrey did the morning show for CBS. John Gambling did WOR's. NBC, with a jumble of fifteen minutes from Chicago, twenty-five minutes from Washington, five minutes of news, fifteen minutes with Robert Q. Lewis, ran a poor third. This is not the answer to morning radio. As I discovered from people like Clint Buehlman—probably one of the most radio-wise persons I've ever encountered—personality is everything. Clint was the man to listen to in Buffalo. You got up in the morning, had coffee and rolls, orange juice and Buehlman. You wouldn't do without the rolls or the juice or the coffee or Buehlman.

CBS had Godfrey. WOR had Gambling. NBC had a problem, but they also had Johnny Murphy. He started in the business as an NBC page boy, and had advanced to the Station Relations department by the time we crossed paths. Shortly after, he left NBC to join the Crosley Broadcasting Corporation in Dayton, Ohio. With Crosley, he gave Phil Donahue his first TV talk show. I'm fortunate Johnny stayed with NBC as long as he did.

Acting as liaison between NBC and their Buffalo affiliate, WBEN, Johnny apparently suggested me as NBC's answer to Godfrey and Gambling, and without my knowledge took an audio recording of my show back to NBC. NBC invited me to New York. Of course I said yes—this being easily the biggest break of my life up to that moment. Bob Thompson wished me farewell with a parting thought: "Look, Bob, if you want to go to New York, you have my blessings. I'll just tell you one thing. You're a big fish in this town. I hope you don't get lost in the big city. I certainly want more than two or three cars in my funeral procession."

I thanked him and conferred with Mil. She said, "Absolutely. You've got to do it." She knew that if I turned it down, I'd spend the rest of my days wondering what would have happened if I'd gone. I couldn't live with that question over my head, and I'd never get another chance like it. So we packed the kids and the turtles and the goldfish in our little Ford and followed the moving van to New York, to a home we'd picked out on Paine Avenue in New Rochelle. Paine Avenue got its name from Revolutionary War firebrand Thomas Paine's cherry orchard in which it nestled and from the Thomas Paine cottage at the end of the street. Inside the cottage, still standing, sat an unnervingly lifelike wax statue of Paine, poised at his desk.

WEAF's Jim Gaines became my boss. He started me on the air from 7:00 to 8:30 A.M. then backed me up to 6:30, then to 6:00, giving me what in 1946 constituted a fabulous deal: a guaranteed $750 a week plus commissions. Commissions tied in to the number of sponsors I could attract and how much the sponsors were prepared to pay to advertise on our show. We soon completely sold out—in other words, had as many sponsors as we could handle without dropping one in favor of another. The longer I had on the air, the higher the commissions rose, into astronomical figures. I earned them—

if only because doing the show meant my waking at 4:15 A.M. and driving into the city from Westchester County on a daily basis. On the other hand, it was a different New York City then. Traffic whizzed along. You got around in one-tenth the time it takes today. It was lovely, sane, safe, not a zoo. And of course, it was the hub of the industry. Radio, advertising, and such as it was, TV.

I came to Jim with two requests that to me were tantamount to demands, only because I valued them so totally. I asked to have the same engineer each day, and I asked for a cough box.

Why? And what?

I wanted the same engineer each day, and I wanted him to be a good record player. By this I mean that he had to be able to spot records and begin them exactly where I wanted. For instance, if we had a recording of Dinah Shore's "Buttons and Bows" and it had a four-bar introduction before she sang, maybe I preferred not to use the four bars. I'd had great success in Buffalo with playing my own introductions on the piano, singing an intro, and—let's say she sang in the key of D-flat—I'd play and sing, then say "Come on, Dinah, you take it," hit a nice A-flat bell note, and she'd come right in, boom, on cue. To accomplish this, I needed a pro at the controls. And because we'd rehearse the next day's show after each show ended in the morning—running through the

records we'd do next time, working out how I'd piano modulate into them—it had to be the same pro Monday through Saturday.

Lady Luck really smiled on me when they gave me Jack Petry. A summer replacement engineer, he was far from being the likeliest choice. But we hit it off beautifully from the beginning—so much so that I really hit the ceiling when I showed up the first Saturday and someone else took his place.

"Where's Jack?"

"He works Monday through Friday. We'd have to pay him overtime to come in today."

"If you don't, I will." I'm told steam rose out of my ears when I said this. "Saturday is just as important as Monday through Friday. Maybe more important. I might have an audience on Saturday that I don't draw on a weekday. You want me to do Saturday with an engineer who hasn't rehearsed the show?"

No one conceded easily, but at long last I won. Then Jack and I had a ball. We even did our record tricks with commercials. We had Holt Deland, the car dealers on Broadway and 56th, as one of our sponsors. On the air I'd say, "Oh, here's Vaughn Monroe." I'd deepen my voice to sound like his and say hello back to myself. I'd continue, "Vaughn, do you know that special song for Holt Deland? Will you sing it for us?" I'd say yes in his voice, hit an arpeggio, and croon, "When you want a car, a used car that is grand, go see Henry Holt or Bob Deland. Then take your girlie to the—"

On this cue Jack would come in on the vocal with Vaughn singing his number-one hit song "Dance, Ballerina, Dance" on the phonograph, and it sounded like Vaughn did the whole pitch.

Jack remained with me for the duration of my tenure on the radio program. Many years later I prevailed upon him to come to television and work with us on *The Howdy Doody Show*. He started with playing the recorded speeches for the puppets, then served as floor manager, associate and assistant director, and finally as one of our best directors. Graduating Doodyville, he became Perry Como's unit manager, the head of all unit managers at NBC, and ultimately a power to be reckoned with in Standards and Practices. Before he retired he'd been promoted to Vice President of NBC in charge of Standards and Practices. We're still best of friends.

Concerning the cough box, I'd had one in Buffalo and never even considered working without one in New York, although we didn't call it a cough box back home, because we didn't have to. The box sat on the piano music rack. It had a switch with three positions. In the middle position, the switch turned the mike off. In the down position, the microphone went on. In the up position, the mike only broadcast as far as the control room,

enabling me to communicate with the engineer without the audience hearing it. The idea was that if I was on the air about to do a Super Suds commercial, I'd hit the switch to up, say "Cue Super Suds" to the engineer in the control room, then tap it down for "The time is exactly eight minutes past eight."

When I asked for the box, I got a no: "You're interfering with the job of a NABET [National Association of Broadcasting Engineers and Technicians] man."

"I'm not," I replied. "You'll still have an engineer. I'm not going to take his job away."

"The union specifies that you can't turn a mike on and off unless you're an engineer."

Then inspiration struck: "What if I have to cough? Call it a cough box. If I'm talking and I have to cough, I'll just switch it off. Otherwise, when I have to cough, I have to get the engineer's attention and signal him by making cutting motions under my chin. What if he's distracted in the booth? What if *he's* coughing? I'm supposed to gag while I try to catch his eye?"

Finally—certainly not immediately: "Okay, you'll have your cough box."

To my knowledge, there isn't a professional studio in the world today that doesn't have a cough box of this sort, controlled by the performer. And I don't recall anyone using one before

I did in 1946.

Those were the glory days of radio. We'd sing, do patter, play musical instruments, and spin records. We did things that I'm sure sound dated now, but only because they wouldn't go over on television. Believe me, they're still fun on radio.

What am I talking about? For one thing, Arthur and his pinochle game. I had a prop phone in the studio, and I'd dial while I did my patter. "Well, let's see who's at the weather bureau today. Oh, hi, Sonny. You gonna be there all day? Isn't that nice. Uh-huh. And tomorrow you're leaving. Cloudy's due in tomorrow? Well, say hello for me, will you? We've been fortunate. He hasn't been around for weeks. Will he be there all day? Oh—partly. I see. Sonny, what's the official temperature? Sixty-five? Oh, pardon me, I want to see what Arthur says."

Then I'd walk to the window in the studio and I'd say, "Hello, Artie. Hey, buddy. What's that? Sixty-eight?" And then I'd tell the audience, "Arthur says sixty-eight just now. . . . [Pause] . . . Who's Arthur? Oh, that's Arthur Mometer outside my studio window. Arthur's always a little higher. That's from all the hot air blowing out of the studio."

It might sound silly, but I liked it enough to borrow it from Clint Buehlman. Before I left Buffalo, I asked him if he'd mind my taking Arthur to New York. He told me travel would do Arthur a world of good. So Arthur tagged along, and I'd get letters from the audience like "Best to you and Arthur and Jack Petry."

Another routine I often used was "It's going to be beautiful today. Mother, you can hang out." With this, I'd explain that my mom never cared if it rained from Tuesday to Sunday, as long as Monday was nice for hanging out. Laundry, that is. She loved being able to get through the washing and ironing on Monday, which meant starting at six in the morning and wrapping up at midnight. If it didn't rain, she could wash and wring out the clothes, carry them from the basement to the ground floor—instead of all the way up to the attic—and hang them out to dry. Women across the country were in precisely the same spot as Mom and knew exactly what I meant by "You can hang out."

I hadn't been out of Buffalo too long when Arthur Godfrey quit his local New York radio show to do a network program, 10:00 to 11:00 A.M. Jack Sterling replaced Godfrey, and where I'd had an uphill struggle against the unbeatable Godfrey, I was able to put a major dent in Jack's ratings. For several time segments I had the number-one rated morning show in New York.

Behind the scenes at NBC, at least six other people thought they should have the show instead of me. If I'd had the knife concession outside my office, I'd have made more money than I got doing the program. Newscaster Charles F. McCarthy—"Don't call me Charlie, I'm not Edgar Bergen's puppet"—imagined himself to have a monopoly on quirky weather broadcasts. His "McCarthy's Unofficial Weather Forecast" had plenty of fans. He'd say, for instance, "This is a trolley wire day." That would mean it's windy, because men used to have a wire or cord running from their coat lapels up to their hats to keep the hats from blowing off on windy days. When I came from Buffalo, Charles F. took tremendous objection to Arthur Mometer and mother hanging out.

Pretty soon Jim Gaines had me in his office: "Charles doesn't like you giving the weather right before he comes on at seven-thirty."

I protested, "Isn't it the greatest service I can provide in the morning— giving time and weather and dangerous road conditions, school closings, isn't that what the radio is for? Are we supposed to wait around for half an hour for 'the unofficial weather forecast' at a quarter to eight from His Highness?"

Jim said okay, and Charles didn't speak to me for three weeks. But once we got to talking again, we buried the hatchet. Charles had a great sense of humor, told fabulous stories, and was fun to be around.

Of course, radio had its share of bloopers. Tex and Jinx Falkenberg had the slot following mine. Their producer used to give my producer a slip of paper in the control room, indicating the names of their guests for me to billboard.

One morning I stepped out into the hall for water. When I returned, the slip of paper was waiting for me, advising that Dana Andrews would be on Tex and Jinx's show. Since I began my day at 4:15 in the morning, I didn't have very much contact with the rest of the world. The only two Danas I knew were girls. Reading Dana's name, I told the listeners that while the last record was playing, I went out into the hall to the drinking fountain and saw Tex and Jinx's guest, Dana Andrews, "and is she gorgeous. Make sure you stay tuned to Dana, because she's a knockout!" The control booth erupted in laughter. Next day, the mail poured in. Some letters accused me of insanity. But one man wrote, "My wife loves him. That'll fix her!"

You hear a story like this and you're bound to wonder "Did Bob Smith live in a cave?" The answer is that I might as well have, because I had all these hours each week to fill and had to concentrate my efforts pretty much on filling them. I did have the assistance of a superb secretary in Muriel Byrne, whose brother was Brendon Byrne, former governor of New Jersey. Along with clerical and related chores, she did the programming for me.

When we needed another hand, we turned to a capable, outgoing NBC page who sat at the desk by the fourth-floor elevator. Young men vied for the post of NBC page if they had any aspirations to be in radio or television. Consequently, pages had to step aside to make room for new hopefuls after six months.

This particular page, Bobby Keeshan, approached me one day with an intriguing proposition: "My six months are up soon. Can I work for you?"

"What do they pay you here?"

"Forty dollars. I'd be glad to work for you for the same money."

"Great, Bobby, you're on!" At the end of his six months, he joined me and proved invaluable. For one thing, he handled the song pluggers. Anyone who had a radio show that did any sort of music with as much airtime as I had couldn't avoid being surrounded by them. I'd walk down the street. Five or six or seven would fall into step, following me, promoting their tunes. So I hired Bobby to deal with them, help with programming, and in general serve as my office manager. He did a great job. Naturally, we had no idea then that he'd go on to be Clarabell and Captain Kangaroo, just as I had not the slightest inkling that Buffalo Bob Smith would ever pal around with a fellow named Howdy Doody.

Shortly after, I added Vic Campbell to the staff. He'd been a good writer and announcer back when I first knew him in Buffalo when he, Clint Buehlman, and I worked together, then he joined the army, ultimately serving in General Douglas Mac-

Arthur's radio command. I ran into him in Hurley's, that favorite media hangout on 49th Street and Sixth Avenue, and was happy to find him available to write for my morning show.

Enoch Light—the celebrated band leader of Enoch Light and the Light Brigade—contacted us one day with a cute specialty song called "Where Is Sam?" Did I like it? Sure did. Would I sing it on the air? Couldn't wait. I had wonderful fun with the song on the morning show, enough to want to cut it as a record. I proposed this to Enoch: "How do I go about doing a record of this?"

Enoch responded, "What do you mean?"

We put our heads together comparing contacts, then went to Jim Gaines, inasmuch as RCA owned both the National Broadcasting Company and Victor Records. Victor released the record, even including me as one of the writers. But rather than use *Bob Smith*, I asked them to dub me Sam Hunter (what is it they say about the correlation between bad puns and overtaxed minds)?

I'd like to say the record sold a million copies and went gold. But I'd be kidding. It did no better than acceptably, but it did introduce me to a new facet of the entertainment business, as well as to Enoch Light and one of the song's writers, Edward G. Kean.

Eddie Kean and I became particularly friendly. So young then, and so

HOWDY AND ME

Eddie Kean at the piano. (Courtesy of ☞
Harvey Bilt)

sharp. I dubbed him "The Kid." I hired him as an additional writer, to come up with special bits for my radio show. I could have used nine writers. Two and a half hours a day can eat up material like mad.

I started at WEAF in August 1946. A little under a year later, in March of 1947, Jim Gaines called me into his office to announce a series of children's programs slated for Saturday morning, 9:00 to noon. He had me in mind for 9:30 to 10:00, at $100 a show. I thought, "This will pay for one of my writers," because I'd been paying for them from my pocket.

Vic Campbell and I devised a show called *The Triple B Ranch*, the three Bs to stand for Big Brother Bob. A quiz program, it featured four children

from one grammar school competing against four from another. We used clever, funny, cute questions as opposed to "What's the capital of Illinois?" Comedy questions. The kids sat on wooden horses until one of them missed an answer, whereupon we'd "knock" the boy or girl from the horse, accompanied by appropriate rodeo jargon. "Oooh, the bucking bronco is going to throw you!" Words along those lines.

Four children from each school would compete as friends cheered them on from the audience. They had fun, and I did, but Vic Campbell envisioned even more hilarity. "Bob," he asked out of the blue, "do you do voices? The show has a Western flavor. Let's do a character and make him

your ranch hand."

I stepped into the control room and tried a few different approaches for Vic. The most ridiculous, a Mortimer Snerd-ish country bumpkin type, held certain potential. The voice became "Elmer." Elmer, something of an oaf, had a limited conversational repertoire.

I'd say, "Hiya, Elmer."

He'd respond, "Oh, hoho, howdy doody. Yuh hohoho. Kyuk. Howdy doody."

We'd follow with corny heehaw-type jokes. When we finished the exchange, I'd say so long and he'd answer, "Well, howdy doody. Huh hohoho."

Kids at home took a liking to Elmer. When they came to compete on *Triple B Ranch*, they had their hearts set on seeing him. Because *Triple B* was radio, I didn't need an actual Elmer. I just talked to myself in two voices. Kids would leave the set disappointed: "Aw, where's Howdy Doody?"

This gave us two ideas.

Let's not call him Elmer any more. Let's call him Howdy Doody. It's a cuter name.

And if the kids want to see Howdy Doody, let's put Howdy Doody on TV.

In 1947 virtually everything the industry knew about television, radio had taught us. Early TV was, all in all, little more than radio with a view. In 1947 I'd been in radio for almost twenty years.

2

HOWDY COME, HOWDY GO

*A*ctually, I knew a little more about television than that. Very shortly after I moved to New York City in 1946, Jim Gaines made sure that RCA sent me a television set. Every night our family watched whatever was on, and I often thought how nice it would be to schedule a kids' show for the late-afternoon slot. We watched Bob Emory's *Small Fry* with our children. It was fine, but so low-budget that I couldn't help recognizing the vacuum that existed in children's programming.

In early December of 1947, I walked into Jim Gaines's office with this in mind. There I met a very handsome, friendly gentleman named Martin Stone. I'd seen Marty on television every Sunday doing *Author Meets the Critics*, his own show. Its format consisted of a panel of critics confronting an author, pro and con, reviewing the writer's most recent literary effort. Some nights it could be downright exciting. Although Marty didn't host the series, he did appear at the end of each program to hype the next week's guests, so I felt as if we'd already met. I greeted him with words to this effect, and he returned the compliment by asking me to record a little birthday surprise for his daughter Judy. I liked and admired him, and readily obliged.

Marty had great connections for opening doors in television. He not only had *Author Meets the Critics*, but also *Americana*, a TV quiz for unusually intelligent high schoolers. He asked me, "Hey, what about putting Howdy Doody on television?" Good start. We proceeded to see programming heads Warren Wade and Owen Davis, Jr. Marty waxed eloquent to them about *The Triple B Ranch*, suggesting that they listen to it on radio with the idea of bringing it to TV.

Warren and Owen must have listened the following Saturday, because we got together again within a matter of days. They'd wanted to do something for children before I ever brought it up, using puppets by Frank Paris of *Toby and the Circus*. Additionally, NBC had acquired a huge library of Ben Turpin, Charlie Chase, and other silent comedies from early film producers. They proposed that I host it, preside over games, contests, and music, provide commentary for the movies, and commission Frank to make a Howdy Doody puppet.

We had another meeting. This time I met Roger Muir, probably one of only two or three producers they had in television then. He'd produce for us. I couldn't have been more thrilled. With a definite go-ahead on the table, I naively asked, "For when?"

They said, "Saturday."

I said, "Whuh? Today's Tuesday."

They said, "We'll go on the air from five to six in the evening."

Okay. Radio had taught us to be inventive. We improvised. Eddie Kean, Vic Campbell, Roger, and I kicked around ideas. Our Howdy puppet wouldn't be ready for weeks, but we launched our first TV hour as *Puppet Playhouse* on December 27, 1947, the day after New York City's famous blizzard. We were the first program of the day, preceded only by a geometric test pattern; we remained the first program in many markets for years, with nothing more than those day-long test patterns for a lead-in. In our studio eight boys and girls sat in the Fun House—it had not yet become the Peanut Gallery—in folding chairs. They called me "Mr. Smith," and we featured Frank Paris with his *Toby and the Circus* puppets, old-time movies, and stunts for the youngsters. For guests, we had the Gaudschmidt Brothers with their French poodles, one of the undying acts of vaudeville. Every time one or both of the brothers turned around, their dogs attacked them, knocking them down. The kids loved it. Nonstop hilarity.

The hour went smoothly, landing a glowing *Variety* review that stated we'd be around for years and years because "NBC has the answer to the perfect babysitter, Bob Smith." Originally, as I understand it, NBC considered testing me the first week, Ed Herlihy the second week, and ventriloquist Paul Winchell with his dummy, Jerry Mahoney, the third week. After the third week they'd choose a host. But thanks to *Variety*, I had a permanent job right away.

When we first started—and for

quite a while thereafter—we had no script. We had program outlines at most. Roger and Eddie and I would sit in one of the rooms at NBC, kicking ideas around. As we came up with bits and key words, Bobby Keeshan wrote them down on cue cards. As a procedure evolved and we became more tightly scripted, our dialogue would be printed in black on the cue cards, with different colored lines drawn through each to signify the speaker. Dilly was green. Mr. Bluster was brown. Clarabell's actions were boxed in blue. Mine would be black letters with no colored line. Howdy's would be black with a red line through them. Because Howdy was prerecorded, instead of putting down his entire speech, we just had the last few words down as a cue. It really impressed me years later when Scott and Edie Brinker found us a typewriter keyboard hooked up to a gizmo that printed in gigantic letters, creating wonderful cue cards that no longer had to be lettered by hand. When I went to California a few years back to do our Howdy Doody fortieth anniversary special, the cue card fellows asked what sizes I wanted the letters—two inches, three inches— and produced cards in which the letters were executed in different colors. Red letters. Green letters. Brown letters. Such amazing progress since our humble beginnings!

Compared to the way we started *The Howdy Doody Show*, it was the difference between an Apollo shuttle and a Frisbee. In the beginning we were very much an ad-libbed show.

"Rehearsals" would consist largely of my prescreening the old-time silent movies, making up funny names for the characters; and the organist and sound-effects man prescreening them to plot out background music and noise. When I say I made up names, I'm actually giving myself too much credit. In truth, I borrowed them—from people in Buffalo. It was my way of greeting the folks back home. For instance, the Tons of Fun were three immense configurations of human anatomy that together must have weighed a thousand pounds. They went by the billing "Tons of Fun," but I added my own identifications. They became Buffalo Vic, Buffalo Clint, and Buffalo Bullets. Buffalo Vic took his name from my brother Vic; Buffalo Clint acknowledged my debt to and regard for Clint Buehlman; and Buffalo Bullets signified my oldest brother, Elvin, whom we called Bullets for his fleetfootedness. He couldn't outleg a statue.

A blond actress who frequented these films became Hulda Honnewinkle, lifting the name of a woman in Buffalo's Ladies Aid Society of Emmaus Lutheran Church. Mom, as president of the chapter, laughed and squirmed at the same time, preparing herself for the ribbing she'd get at the meetings and at church each Sunday. A few years into *The Howdy Doody Show*, Hulda married in real life. Her new name: Hulda Honnewinkle Hein-naman. I couldn't wait to use it on the show.

I snatched the name of my good pal Franny Hines for a Charlie Chap-lin–type actor, Bobby Dunne. Peter Gust, who ran the Park Lane Restau-rant, one of the nicest in Buffalo, saw his name employed on each and every occasion that a character cooked in one of these movies. I used Charlie Schwictenberg's name, Adolf Wol-lenschlager's, and Bertha Schlegel's. Bertha, another of my mother's La-dies Aid friends, sat behind us in church in Buffalo and sang lower than any man in the congregation. She had married a Bruno. Whenever we had a funny couple in the films, the kids knew without my telling them that the two would be Bruno and Bertha.

Kids all across the country quickly learned these names. When-ever I ran a silent movie, I could call out, "Who's this? Who's that?" and a studio full of little voices would holler at the tops of their lungs, "Whee! Bruno and Bertha! Yippee! Hulda Honnewinkle Heinnaman! Yaaaaay! Buffalo Vic, Buffalo Clint, and Buffalo Bullets!!!" People congratulated me for coming up with such funny names, and I'd say, "If you think the names are funny, you should know the people."

Though we lacked a puppet that first week, we nonetheless had Howdy by claiming he wouldn't come out of my desk drawer. I sat behind a desk. We trained one of the cameras on the drawer. I said we had Howdy with us, then spoke to him. "You in there, Howdy?"

Then I covered my mouth to muf-fle the sound and answered, "Yuh hoho, yeah, huh, I'm here, but I'm too bash-ful to come out. Kyuk ho ho ho ho."

I kept talking to Howdy all through the show, but of course he never did get up the nerve to step out.

We did the same the following Saturday, and into the third Saturday. When Frank Paris finished Howdy, I began the hour by talking to the drawer anyway. Then it opened at the propitious moment. Howdy, no longer bashful, took his first peek at the American public. The American public caught its first glimpse of him. The children ooohed and aaahed.

I must say now, in retrospect, this Howdy had to be the ugliest puppet imaginable. Frank had fashioned him to resemble the bumpkin voice. The resulting fellow looked as feeble-minded as a puppet can look without drooling. The kids, however, imme-diately adored him.

At first, we aired our TV show only on Saturdays. Later we added Thursdays, then Tuesdays. Not sur-prisingly, this confused parents and children, particularly little folks too young to understand calendars and days of the week. Children, quick to make parents' lives a living hell when things confuse them, demanded to know why they couldn't watch Howdy on Monday, Wednesday, and Friday.

Here I am with the first Howdy Doody in March 1948, announcing that our show will go to five times a week.

Roger Muir noted that our own lives could also be tidier if we had to prepare only a half-hour program each day, instead of killing ourselves to turn out two and three hour-long shows a week. He proposed Monday-to-Friday half hours, 5:30 to 6:00, targeting the time when we assumed most kids were coming indoors while Mommy cooked dinner.

It may seem trivial now, but then it made headlines. Radio had weekly shows. TV didn't. When NBC concurred with Roger in spring 1948, they made *The Howdy Doody Show* their first Monday-to-Friday daily show. I remember building up to the announcement. The big news was five. We were going to be on five times a week. We had fives all over the set.

We learned a lot those first years, learned by doing. Under primitive conditions. Radio was the recognized broadcast giant. TV was "Hey, Mickey, hey, Judy, let's put on a show in the barn!" If we needed an extra piano for the set, we had to convince the radio people to lend us one. We

HOWDY COME, HOWDY GO

I know it's 1949 and I'm explaining a turret lens in NBC's Studio 3B, but I've forgotten who the Indians are. Maybe they're distant relations (through my ties with the Sigafoose tribe).

shared our studio with other programs' sets, meaning that when Howdy went off at six on Tuesday and Thursday, the cameramen swung the monstrously heavy equipment around and wheeled it to the other end of the room for *The Roberta Quinlan Show* and "CARpets from the looms of Mohawk! CARpets for your rooms by Mohawk!" On Monday, Wednesday, and Friday, the same cameras shot the same part of the studio during the same time slot but for another show, that of Morton Downey (Sr.) For a while we had John Cameron Swayze's *Camel News* across from us.

I stand corrected. We weren't Mickey and Judy putting on a show in the barn. We were Mickey and Judy putting on a show in Grandma's attic. Incidentally, one of our floor managers in the early years was Nick Dunne. Today he's the bestselling novelist Dominick Dunne.

Roger—whose presence of mind, diplomacy, and sheer strategical genius pulled us through more crises than I'll ever be able to thank him for—recalls our rudimentary learning

HOWDY AND ME

experiences as "a lot of fumbling. We really didn't know what we were doing, but we had a built-in research operation, and that was the Peanut Gallery. If the kids reacted positively to something, we were on the right track. If they didn't, we found out why, or reworked or abandoned it. The Peanut Gallery functioned for us much the way comedy clubs do in the present day and age."

One bad habit heads the list of practices we had to rethink. Since I'm not a ventriloquist, I move my lips when I talk for Howdy. It didn't matter on radio, because I could cover my mouth with my hand for the benefit of the kids in the studio, and radio listeners didn't see me. Nor did it matter with Howdy in the drawer. I could still cover my mouth. But once Howdy stood up and we had conversations, I couldn't be pawing at my face all the time. Of course, I could speak freely when we had the camera on Howdy alone in a one-shot—until we discovered that it bewildered the kids. They stared from me to Howdy, Howdy to me, me to Howdy. Once they mastered the mystery, they had shattered illusions as their reward. That's when I started recording some of Howdy's speeches in advance.

I didn't always prerecord them. When I didn't have to be onstage with Howdy, I went backstage and did the voice live. This allowed greater spontaneity. As our cast grew, we did this with every character. First thing each day, we'd mark the puppet speeches we wanted to prerecord, then recorded them with two seconds of silence between speeches. During the show, the engineer would let the speech run until its conclusion, then stop the record with his finger. (I told you we were primitive.) When we needed the next recorded speech, the engineer lifted his finger.

Early television, like radio, did not automatically take to the airwaves with a complete roster of sponsors. We had to sell the slots one by one. Sponsors had ample evidence that newspaper and magazine ads sold products and that a popular radio show could command incredible audience loyalty. But television? Worse, television scheduled too early in the evening for the whole family to watch? In these days before ratings points and Nielsen families, a series' success could best be measured by how many sponsors grabbed it how soon. Yet agencies had only to see statistics to prove that, thus far, television couldn't even sell television sets. Fifty-six million people had radios. Fewer than twenty thousand possessed TVs.

NBC's sales department needed proof that we had selling power. It was 1948, an election year, so Eddie Kean came up with the notion that Howdy Doody would run for "President of all the kids in the United States." He wrote a song:

Howdy Doody for President.
He's America's choice.
He will never be hesitant
To fight for the rights of girls and
boys.
Howdy Doody for President.
In the White House he'll be.
Howdy Doody for President.
Let's speed him on to victory.

Arrangement © Edward G. Kean and
Robert E. Smith, 1987

I'm convinced. Aren't you? If General Dwight D. Eisenhower hadn't led the Allied Forces to victory in World War II—and if kids had had the vote—Howdy would have defeated Ike that year. We had the campaign. We had the enthusiasm. We had airtime on the full NBC network—all of six stations, because this preceded the coaxial cable that eventually linked East and West. The full NBC network consisted of New York City, Boston, Schenectady, Philadelphia, Washington, and Baltimore.

Roger suggested that we offer free buttons. We had 10,000 made—statistically, enough for 50 percent of all the TV sets in the country. Any child who wanted to vote for our candidate could send in a self-addressed, stamped envelope and in return get this button with a picture of our goofy-looking Howdy Doody. It read "I'm for" above the picture and "Howdy Doody" below it.

"The strategy," says Roger, "was foolproof and simple. Ha. I had no doubt that the seven secretaries at NBC-TV could send out buttons in their downtime. We made a pitch on Saturday evening. Powie. Tuesday morning we barely walked into the building when I got a call, 'What the hell did you guys do? You sabotaged the mailroom. We've got bags and bags of mail, most of it for your buttons. How are we supposed to find the real mail? How are we supposed to conduct business?' "

We had 2,200 letters from Boston, 5,400 from Philadelphia, 8,600 from New York. I didn't know whether to say "Oh boy!" or "Uh-oh!" We hadn't ordered nearly enough buttons. I figured I'd either be fired or would have to pay for new buttons from my own pocket. Roger went up to see John F. Royal, NBC-TV's unofficial resident showman and first vice president in charge of television. After demanding and hearing the full story, John had a few suggestions of his own. "Okay, it was a good plan. But you made mistakes. First, you should not have had them write to NBC. You should have gotten a post office box. Second, seven secretaries can't handle this mail. You have to turn it over to a commercial fulfillment operation. Once you've done that, do maybe three more pitches and let's see how it goes."

We pulled a quarter of a million responses. The sales department jumped for joy, because we'd demonstrated a phenomenal number of children glued to each TV set in NBC's

Niles Trammell, who was NBC, believed in the potential of Howdy and me from the beginning—and even when our success made it harder for him to get show tickets.

six markets. Based on those figures, they were able to go out and sell our impact to major sponsors.

Our very first, not a mass-market product in the least, had been Pioneer Scientific—a screen pressed over people's glass TV screens to cut down glare. Another early one was Unique Art Toy Company, which made a wind-up toy of me at the piano and Howdy dancing.

But hot on the heels of the button

bonanza, Howdy began to attract blue-chip backers. Niles Trammell, president of NBC, had terrific contacts with many of the largest companies in the United States, among them the Colgate Palmolive Peat Company. Niles got in touch with Ed Little, chairman of the board of Colgate. The only man I ever knew who called Mr. Little by his first name, Niles said, "Ed, we have a show here for you. I predict we'll sell more toothpaste than anything you could possibly buy."

Colgate's took a chance on us, be-

HOWDY COME, HOWDY GO ———————

coming one of our truly great and favorite sponsors. A whole generation learned about dental care whenever Mr. Tooth Decay threatened Happy Tooth; and they sat in smug anticipation as a golfer whacked a ball at the head of an announcer, because they knew that a pane of glass stood between the green and the endangered cranium. The announcer would go on to explain that Colgate's "invisible shield" protected teeth the same way.

Other sponsors followed Colgate's lead. Before long, we completely sold out our available commercial time. Even at that, we turned down several possibilities that Roger, NBC, or I thought inappropriate for children. We insisted on quality and rejected products not in the best interests of our audience.

Although we were "only" TV, our esteem rose in NBC's eyes. We achieved enough autonomy to have our own people, our own self-contained group, and isolated offices toward the back of the sixteenth floor at 30 Rockefeller Plaza. We were all on NBC's staff, but we operated essentially as an independent unit.

Marty Stone, who had an excellent eye for business, took me under his wing. He became my manager, my attorney, almost my godfather. He made sure that I owned the Howdy Doody name and character. One day a toy buyer from Macy's stopped by the set during a rehearsal, eager to examine Howdy. He told us the stores had been getting calls for a Howdy doll.

Frank Paris, who brought Howdy to the studio every day in a cloth bag and took him home every night, heard the conversation. He assumed he'd receive a royalty. NBC informed him that he had accepted $500 outright for making the puppet. He felt otherwise, insisting on a share of the action. Marty and I met with NBC, then with Frank Paris and his attorney. We offered Frank a job as our number-one puppeteer for as long as we remained on the air, period. NBC reasserted that they had paid him for making the puppet and that the name, character, and concept had existed before he ever began to give it wooden form.

Frank disagreed. He packed up his Howdy in that cloth bag and went home. He walked out of 30 Rock and we never saw either that Howdy or Frank Paris again. It was one in the afternoon. We had a show to do in four and a half hours. Now what?

Once in the studio, we told Eddie Kean the story. Eddie had the inspiration that if Howdy Doody was running for President of All the Kids in the United States, it stood to reason that he was running against somebody. He proposed a rival for Howdy—the handsome Mr. X—and that Howdy decided he'd better have a facelift, or risk losing the votes of all the girls. That's what I announced on the show that night. "But don't worry, kids. It's not a bad operation.

It won't hurt him. It's just that Howdy won't be with us until he completes his surgery."

As a historical aside, it's been pointed out to me that the senior kids in this audience were old enough to vote when the young, strikingly attractive John F. Kennedy ran against Eisenhower's Vice President, Richard Nixon, in 1960. If there's any connection, I disavow it emphatically. The power of suggestion? Who, us?

In early TV, our only vision of the future was tomorrow or next week. While Howdy went under the knife, we went to work on another Howdy. Norman Blackburn, an NBC vice president recently arrived from the West Coast, put us in touch with two animation artists from the Walt Disney Studios. We asked them for a good-looking, ten-year-old, all-American boy whose appearance went with the way Howdy's voice sounded. His voice, incidentally, had changed by then to one less dopey and more boyish than at first—simply because, when Howdy started singing, I couldn't make it work in his original register. I had to bring him up in pitch.

The two artists came up with several renderings of a new Howdy and rushed them to New York. Roger, Warren Wade, Norman Blackburn, Bobby Sarnoff, and I met to consider the various versions. (Bobby, son of General David Sarnoff who created the NBC network, began in the NBC sales department. One of his first assignments was to sell *The Howdy Doody Show*. In later years, his assignments would include the roles of president and chairman of NBC.) Finally we selected the head from one, the body from another, mixing and matching details. We sent the composite to Velma Dawson, a fine sculptor and puppetmaker also with the Disney Studios. Velma made the actual puppet. We hired Rhoda Mann, who had worked for Frank Paris, to operate him.

All along we had a show to do. Kids worried about Howdy. Is he okay? Why does surgery last so long? I prerecorded his voice each day, then spoke to him on the air on the Super Talk-O-Scope. He'd tell us about the hospital, and how he was fine, didn't mind plastic surgery, and knew he'd get the girls' votes now that he'd be handsome too. In other words, we stalled and stalled.

This appeased the kids, but not the sponsors. They wanted Howdy in the commercials and not just on the Super Talk-O-Scope. Eddie Kean rose to the challenge again, suggesting that we find any puppet, dress him appropriately, and bandage his head. The puppet appeared on the air, assuring the boys and girls of his excellent health and the advisability of brushing with Colgate's or whatever.

Now we had happy sponsors. Impatient boys and girls. And a little guy in puppet hospital, waiting for the big unveiling.

3

POPULATING DOODYVILLE

The day we introduced the new Howdy Doody, he began the show with his head swathed in surgical dressing. We continued to build up anticipation for the unveiling, up to the last possible second. At the moment of revelation, I literally felt the thrill in the air. The kids went wild. For myself, I knew what he'd look like and thought I had no surprises in store. He'd be a redhead, his face bright and smiling, full of energetic wonderment and joy, with forty-eight freckles— one for each state in the Union. He wore blue jeans, boots, a big bandanna, a sleeve garter, and a gingham shirt. Something happened, personally, to me, because here stood someone special.

I never accepted the original Howdy Doody as being any more than an object. On the other hand, I've never seen Velma Dawson's Howdy as any less than a young pal. I simply had to relate to this Howdy on a higher level. I won't tell you I ask him for stock tips, or that Howdy and I go for walks in the sunset every evening. That would be ridiculous, and if you believed it, I'd really be in trouble. No, I don't go for strolls with Howdy, and we don't hold lengthy conversations unless we're performing. But I sometimes say good night to him before I turn out the lights in my study, and I do count myself forever lucky to be remembered as his friend.

The unveiling impressed kids,

Here's the definitive Howdy Doody, but ☞ *you'll notice that my costume still had a way to go.*

parents, sponsors, even the press. Billy Rose gave it accolades in his celebrated "Pitching Horseshoes" column. At Marty Stone's urging, I recognized that this Howdy could reach heights far beyond any conceivable for his predecessor. Prior to this point, I'd been getting $100 per show, out of which I paid Eddie Kean to write it and Bobby Keeshan to hold and print cue cards. Not lucrative by a long shot, but this is how people got one foot in the door of the potentially wonderful world of television.

With the new Howdy, Marty negotiated a great contract for me with NBC. To begin with, much more money. Better still, I retained outright ownership of Howdy Doody's name, character, and copyright. I'd paid to have the new Howdy made; I subsequently paid for the making of, and retained the characters and copyrights for, every puppet in Doodyville. I agreed to share royalties with NBC, whose billion-dollar facilities made all the publicity and marketing a reality. I further agreed to split royalties with Marty 50/50, a standard figure at the time, and to split my 50 percent with NBC on the same basis. In other words, if a manufacturer paid me $100,000 to put Howdy's picture on a wristwatch or shirt or toy, Marty got $50,000, NBC $25,000, and Buffalo Bob $25,000. I had no objections. That seemed to be the way it was done.

The royalties rolled in. Doodyville took shape. With early television,

cameras were vastly inferior to those we have today, and the lights were ferociously hot. At the beginning, I just wore slacks and a sports shirt. When we decided that all kids liked circuses, we abandoned the *Puppet Playhouse* format in favor of *The Howdy Doody Circus*. Howdy inherited a circus from his grandpa, and I, as his guardian, accordingly switched to the hardly more sophisticated garb of a lion tamer—pith helmet, riding pants, boots, and a Howdy Doody shirt put out by one of our licensees. It had "Howdy" on one pocket and "Doody" on the other.

From almost no scripting, we got into partial scripting. We still wouldn't script the old-time movies, but we honed in on some sort of theme or plot. Forming Howdy Doody's Circus was the first real story line we had. Then we dumped the writing into Eddie Kean's lap. With five TV shows a week plus radio, I had my hands full, as did Roger and Marty. What would we have done without Eddie? I shudder to imagine. "The Kid" was a master at knowing what was fun for kids and for parents as well. Adults would watch us for the little asides we used to do. From 1947 to 1954, Eddie wrote 125 marvelous songs, seven years of delightful stories, and forever had to bail us out of one after another baleful situation.

For example, the lion tamer routine didn't last long. I got to thinking that I never liked pretending to be an uncle to the boys and girls, or their Big Brother Bob, or using "Mr. Smith" because those titles conferred a sort of distancing respect. Marty thought of naming me Buffalo Bob, then we tossed it into Eddie's lap. Eddie who whipped up one of his tremendous solutions: My uncle, Buffalo Tom, it seems, had been the great white leader of the Sigafoose tribe. In due course, Buffalo Tom went to the happy hunting grounds. The tribe studied its lore to locate his rightful heir. It was me! In a big ceremony on the show, I inherited his rank and his Buffalo Suit, composed of such stylish articles as metal beer coasters strung together for a belt. I was officially named Buffalo Bob and to this day am probably still the great white leader of the Sigafoose Indians.

At first, we had only one live character on the show. Me. Bobby Keeshan handled my cue cards and, not enjoying the blazing lights any more than I did, usually wore only slacks and a white T-shirt. One day we'd had a contest and were running late. Instead of lunging across the floor to get the prizes, I asked Bobby to bring me one. He did, in the process walking into camera range.

Later on, Warren Wade sought me out. A decorated colonel during World War II, he bore certain mannerisms reminiscent of Nigel Bruce's version of Dr. Watson. Warren demanded in a blustery voice, "That fella who walked on camera there with the white T-shirt. Is that good television?"

"Not really, but I was in a hurry."

"Look, if he's going to do this again, let's dress him up as something. Make a character of him."

Here I'm wearing an early version of the Buffalo Suit

We liked the idea. Roger scared up something. Bobby would be a clown, and we'd either have him in polka dots or green-and-white striped zebra fabric. We tried both fabrics on camera, determining that stripes photographed better, then scouted clowns at Ringling Brothers Barnum and Bailey Circus for a sense of what makeup Bobby ought to wear. Ultimately, makeup whiz Dick Smith created for Bobby his soon-to-be world-famous Clarabell cranium—he gave him a bald pate with orange fringe, furnished him with a bulbous nose, painted his face, and created the look that Clarabell kept ever after. Now, if Bobby walked

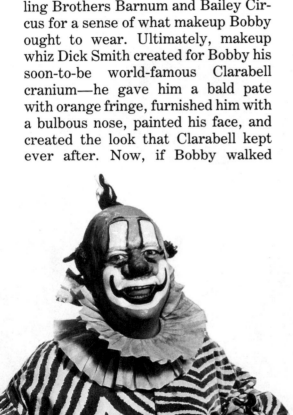

onto camera, at least he looked like a character. If he had to hand me a prop or a prize, I could feel perfectly comfortable saying "Thanks, Bobby." And he could easily and without fear of reproach say "You're welcome."

We thought.

Then Warren Wade approached me with "Hey, that fella with the clown suit."

"Yea—h?"

"He talked."

"So?"

"Don't let him talk. If he talks, we're going to have to pay him union scale."

"Okay, fine."

Then I went to Bobby Keeshan: "Bobby, you don't mind not talking, do you?"

"No, I didn't have anything to say anyway."

We had Bobby dressed like a clown on camera and not talking on camera from the neck up. Instead, he pantomimed. Eddie christened him "Clarabell" because, explained Eddie, "It's a silly name." Eddie then added the idea that since Clarabell, like Harpo Marx, never talked on camera, he would communicate the way Harpo did, with a horn. Our refinement would be that Clarabell had two horns—the happy horn on the right side of his body that meant yes; and the sort of dejected horn on the left,

Bob Keeshan as Clarabell.

HOWDY AND ME

signifying no. Clarabell wore his box over his stomach like a peanut vendor. We wrote "Clarabell" on it and occasionally used it for props like Hostess Twinkies when we did commercials, and for his ever-popular seltzer bottle, the last word in many an argument.

"Clarabell, don't be acting so foolish."

Honk, honk.

"Clarabell, stop that."

Honk, honk.

"Clarabell, do you want me to embarrass you by scolding you in front of the Peanut Gallery?"

Squirt!

Fans have observed that in the legend of the Lone Ranger, only the Ranger's faithful Indian companion Tonto and a woman named Clarabell Hornblower knew his true identity. They've asked whether our Clarabell blew his horns as a pun on Clarabell Hornblower. The answer is no. I never heard of her till the fans told me, and Eddie swears he never heard of her before I told him.

That's how Clarabell came into being. It may not sound like the ideal formula for creating a folk character, but such were the mysterious workings of early television. He didn't talk on the show merely because it started out being cheaper that way. We were halfway through his evolution before we actually planned a single aspect of

Bob Keeshan as the Featherman.

POPULATING DOODYVILLE ——

him—when we started fiddling with his horns and box. To realize how unplanned it all was, just bear in mind that if there had been different fabric or costumes in the wardrobe at NBC, Bobby Keeshan could just as easily have emerged as a fireman, a cowboy, or a kangaroo.

Eventually Bobby wanted to have a speaking part. Eddie Kean thought of the Featherman, for which Bobby dressed as an Indian rather than a clown. Since Chief Featherman and Clarabell couldn't ever be in the same place at the same time, Eddie con-

Phineas T. Bluster.

cocted a feud between them. The Featherman resented the clown in the zebra-striped suit: "Me no like Carbell." Clarabell, petrified, accordingly hid whenever he figured the Featherman might be around. The Featherman lingered only a short while, but he made for a cute, campy bit while he lasted.

Essentially, in the beginning, we had Howdy, we had Clarabell, we had me. We had the circus. We had precious little in the way of conflict, action, and interrelationships, and were light-years away from *Days of Our Lives*. We needed other characters, with contrasting personalities, whose

lives would interweave and furnish stories. In short, what we lacked was a decent heavy, so we introduced Phineas T. Bluster. Mr. Bluster, who eventually became Doodyville's mayor, dedicated his life to trying to snatch the circus and other of life's pleasures away from Howdy. He'd engage in such nefarious activities as buying up all the eggs from Mr. Cobb's general store, simply to prevent Howdy and his pals from holding an Easter egg hunt. Sometimes, when appealed to, he'd give in. More often, he had to be outwitted.

Following our circus theme, we borrowed the "Phineas T." of his name from the flamboyant big-top impresario Phineas T. Barnum. The "Bluster" underscored his bombastic personality—inspired to some small degree by our own Warren Wade. Scott Brinker made this paunchy puppet, using half a volley ball for the stomach. Mr. Bluster wore a suit, a vest, and a watch on a fob. His eyebrows shot heavenward whenever he got into a snit, which happened most of the time. Dayton Allen operated Mr. Bluster and provided his voice. When we decided to make Mr. Bluster one of three triplets, Dayton's puppeteering duties expanded to include Phineas T.'s two brothers, Don José Bluster from South America and Hector Hamhock Bluster from England.

Dayton was just marvelous, certainly one of the funniest persons who ever graced any stage, anywhere, anytime. If somebody could have harnessed that talent, Dayton could have been the next Groucho Marx. When we hired him, we said we had to have a puppeteer who did voices. Dayton replied, "Oh, I've been puppeteering all my life." I don't think he'd ever touched a puppet before that moment, but he got the job and practiced feverishly to learn the skills of the trade. I give him full credit. He absolutely made Mr. Bluster breathe. Perfection.

Over time, Dayton added a few live characters to his repertoire. For Ugly Sam the wrestler, he wore a red-and-white striped old-fashioned bathing suit, the kind that covered the chest and went down to the knees. Sam never won a fight in his life and spoke as if every match had consisted of the opponent stomping poor Sam's head into the mat. Dayton also did Pierre the Chef, with a French accent. Pierre always had some crazy new delicacy to extol and was great to use in commercials.

In Western clothes and a moustache, Dayton played Lanky Lou, the sheriff of Doodyville, loquacious until asked a question—whereupon he went blank. One year, on a show we did the Friday before Mother's Day, Dayton brought his mother to be Lanky Lou's mother. My mother, Emma Kuehn Schmidt, portrayed Buffalo Emma— Buffalo Bob's mom. My brother Vic, my sister Esther, and Mil were backstage to give Mom moral support before the show. Mil had asked her,

"Gee, Gram, are you all right? Are you going to get nervous?" This seventy-year-old phenomenon answered, "Tsk, tsk, honey. Why would I get nervous? I've done plays in church where we had 200, maybe 220 people in the audience. You don't have near that many here." She didn't stop to consider that some 12 million people would be watching her on their home TV sets.

In that episode of the Doodyville saga, we had her out bearhunting. Offstage, of course. As we talked about it, she entered between two cameras, wearing one of my Buffalo Bob costumes and dragging a tremendous stuffed bear. Her first line was "My children will never starve!"

Dayton had another live character, Sir Archibald the English explorer. Sir Archibald wore a pith helmet, khaki shorts and shirt, and spoke very stuffily, veddy uppah crust. For one segment we went tramping through a woodsy set for some expedition. Poll Parrott was one of our sponsors—actually, the Rand Shoe Company of St. Louis. Rand made Poll Parrott shoes for children. Over the years we did umpteen commercials for Poll Parrott. But occasionally we also did spots for Rand Shoes for men, because dads watched us with their kids. So in the course of Sir Archibald's and my expedition, we paused to praise Rand Shoes. Sir Archie wore them because they felt so good on his feet, and he could walk forever, and they never hurt.

I was reading the cue cards, spieling and rhapsodizing. Facing the camera, I lifted Dayton's foot to exhibit this fantastic example of craftsmanship. I turned it. I twisted it. Look here. Look there. Wow, notice this. I don't know why, but I sort of forgot that a portion of Dayton was inside it. Without thinking, I wrenched his shoe toward the outside and kept bending. Wincing, he tried to retain his balance. I had no idea and just went on about the shoe. "Look at the lovely heel." Finally he couldn't stand it. Remaining in character with his Sir Archibald accent, he groaned, "Oooh, ooop. Bob, I don't bend that way." This broke up the studio audience, the crew, and me. When I break up, I go to pieces. I can't

do lines. I can't concentrate. I can't coordinate my lips to form words. I just quake, and either walk off stage or crawl off on my hands and knees.

So I disappeared and left the aching Sir Archibald to finish the show in the woods. Lucky for him, he wore comfortable shoes.

We decided that just as I had Howdy for a pal, Mr. Bluster should have someone. We gave him Dilly Dally, a cute, gullible little go-fer. Dilly was the only puppet who, when frustrated, wiggled his ears. As Bluster's naive accomplice, Dilly would do whatever the old sourpuss asked him, until he realized it was wrong. Then he'd come around to our side. Dilly wore a *D* on his turtleneck shirt. When the big trivia wave hit in the late Sixties, even fanatics constantly missed the question "What does the *D* stand for on Dilly Dally's shirt?" They answered, "Dilly Dally, of course." But it didn't. The story is that Dilly, as water boy for Doodyville High's football team, had earned the privilege of wearing a Doodyville High letter sweater. Bill LeCornec operated Dilly and did his squeaky voice, and his Dilly became one of my favorite characters.

Among Bill's live roles were Doctor Singasong, Oil Well Willie, and Chief Thunderthud of the Ooragnak tribe (kangaroo spelled backward). Bill had a truly fine baritone voice. As Doc-

Dayton Allen as Sir Archibald.

HOWDY AND ME

tor Singasong, he wore a high black silk hat and a morning suit and only spoke in song. Oil Well Willie, a prospector, somewhat took off on Gabby Hayes. In baggy clothes and a raggedy sodbuster hat, he'd amble along, sing with me, and inquire after my health: "How yer doin', Buffaler Bob?"

Bill also had a mellifluous straight voice for such announcements as "And now, for the 2242nd *Howdy Doody Show* starring Howdy Doody and Buffalo Bob Smith." But his forte was undoubtedly Chief Thunderthud, the prime target of Clarabell's practical jokes. For example, the chief might walk in with forty gas balloons. I'd ask if they were for the Peanuts in the Peanut Gallery. While the chief explained, "Kawa no, Buffalo Bob. Me have other plans for balloons . . ." Clarabell would be sneaking behind him with scissors, cutting off the balloons, and distributing them among the kids. Then I'd bawl out the chief.

"Oh, Chief," I'd chide, "aren't you ashamed of yourself? You won't give your balloons to the children, but Clarabell is sharing his right now."

Then the chief would see Clarabell, whirl around and look at the empty string pieces in his own hand, chase after Clarabell, and naturally be rewarded with a face full of seltzer from Clarabell's seltzer bottle.

Thanks to Eddie's inexhaustible

Bill LeCornec as Oil Well Willie.

brain, the chief added a new expression to the language. *Kawabonga.* The chief used it whenever he came to grief. (This became another popular trivia question in the Sixties.) Kids all over the country started using it, and I've seen it in any number of cartoons. It's been in two or three *Peanuts* cartoons at least, and in Hallmark greeting cards. Surfers use it as they head into big waves, and soldiers took it to Vietnam. Lately, the mutant Ninja turtles have taken *our* word all over the place—from the giant screen to the packaging for toaster cakes and beyond.

A harder trivia question, by the way, would be "What did the chief and Princess Summerfall Winterspring

say when things went well?" The answer is *KawaGoopa*. Harder than that, what did the cowardly Chief Thunderchicken chirp when we introduced him a few years later? *Kawa Chicken*.

Some chowderhead started the rumor a few years ago that *Kawabonga* signified a profanity, and that when kids at home muttered *Kawabonga*, they were cursing. Believe me, I'd never teach a kid a secret way to curse, and I certainly have no wish to be remembered in that light. I've spent my whole life respecting kids and my religion. On occasion, I contended with censors for permission to remind children to visit their various houses of worship. I did once join forces with my writers to devise a script laden with sexual double entendres, to prove that censors nitpicked all the wrong things, then overlooked the obvious ones. But the implications of *Kawabonga* were always squeaky-clean. Turning a silly, benign little nonsense phrase into something ugly is the sort of rotten trick Mr. Bluster would pull. Let me assure you that as often as Clarabell may have squirted the chief with seltzer, we never, ever had any cause to wash the chief's mouth out with soap.

On the subject of rumors, I've also heard that we engaged in tasteless, off-color jokes during rehearsals. So? Everyone isn't Alistair Cooke. When you kid around with friends, not every goofy remark spills out as a gem. You know from your own experience that when you're having fun with people you like, the corniest behavior can seem hilarious. I don't feel we ever behaved badly. But I will agree, we got silly. Under pressure, if you don't take steps to lighten the tension, you go nuts.

I welcomed the zaniness. I'm just not too delighted with some of the descriptions of it that are bandied about thirdhand, the strangest being that Phineas T. Bluster used to expose himself during rehearsals. Granted, puppeteer Dayton Allen was and is a wild man, but Mr. Bluster exposing himself? Bluster had nothing below his half-a-volleyball stomach other than crossbars. What's to expose?

Dayton especially had the power to crack me up, to reduce me to a quivering mass of giggles. In fact, I recall plenty of rehearsals when I had to force myself to stop laughing and turn into a boss—"Hey, Dayton, will you cut it out? We've got only an hour before we go on . . ."—because if I didn't, we wouldn't have had a show. This was live TV, with minimal rehearsal time. Eventually and reluctantly we had to admit that every second did count.

And eventually it did add up to a strain. I'd worked six and seven days a week since I was fifteen years old, and I played the organ in church on Sundays, generally two services a morning. In New York City, I'd been waking at 4:15 A.M. Monday through

Saturday, doing the 6:00–8:30 A.M. radio show and *The Howdy Doody Show*, not returning home until 7:30 P.M. I'd never had a vacation. I felt sick. Marty, worried, took me to his doctor. His doctor told Marty, "This guy needs a rest." So in 1948, Mil and I went on the first vacation we ever had. J. Fred Coots, the writer of such marvelous songs as "You Go to My Head," "Santa Claus Is Coming to Town," "Love Letters in the Sand," and "Two Tickets to Georgia," invited us to join him on a two-week South American cruise he'd put together for friends aboard the French liner *De-Grasse*.

Preparing to take my brief leave of Doodyville, I pretaped Howdy's voice for the duration. NBC lined up guest hosts to pinch hit for me—Rex Marshall as Sailor Rex, Jimmy Blaine as Jersey Jim. Familiar to children and adults for any number of programs, Jimmy is probably best remembered today for hosting one that would later follow ours, *The Gumby Show*.

Eddie Kean said, "South America! Great! You're going to South America to bring back a rare animal that's eight animals in one. The Flub-a-Dub."

"I am? The what?"

Eddie then concocted the Flub-a-Dub, a strange, speaking creature with a duck's bill, cat's whiskers, cocker spaniel's ears, giraffe's neck, dachshund's body, seal's flippers, pig's tail, and the memory of an elephant.

The Flub-a-Dub.

"My inspiration," says Eddie, "was our budget. We could only afford one animal puppet. With the Flub-a-Dub, we got our money's worth."

Naturally, we raved about our impending acquisition incessantly on the show, right up until the night before my departure.

Mil and I boarded the *DeGrasse* the next morning, and I couldn't count the number of children who came to see us off. I don't know what I expected, but this amazed me. After the kids left and the ship pulled away from the pier, I became supertourist. I had a camera, my first 16-millimeter camera, and fol-

POPULATING DOODYVILLE —————————

lowed what little instruction I'd gotten from the clerk who sold it to me in the store. But people aboard ship, assuming that I had to be an expert, bombarded me with questions. I answered them, even when I didn't know what I was talking about. I came home with terrific pictures. I only hope my advice didn't ruin too many of theirs. The cruise amounted to one long, lively, lovely party. As promised, I returned from it with the Flub-a-Dub in tow.

At first we didn't use a marionette. The Flub-a-Dub walked along the ground, operated by a flexible cable that Clarabell had trouble manipulating. That version didn't work too well, so we redid the Flub-a-Dub with strings. Dayton Allen worked the strings and gave Flub-a-Dub a wacky voice. Yet even in its first incarnation, our "find" was an instant, smash success.

According to Eddie's scenario, the Flub-a-Dub ate nothing but flowers. Every day we'd have fresh carnations or daisies or snapdragons or roses for his dinner. Suddenly mothers deluged us with phone calls and letters: "Get off that eating flowers kick, will you please? Our kids are in the backyard eating roses. Do you want them to swallow thorns?" Eddie bailed us out. The Flub-a-Dub, it developed, didn't like North American flowers. He only liked South American flowers. Lucky for him, someone introduced his palate to meatballs and spaghetti, his new favorite dish. Eddie gave him a song:

*I want some meatballs, meatballs,
    meatballs
And spaghetti.
I'm always ready, to eat spaghetti.
Because it's iggily wiggily tiggily,
Tiggily, yum, yum, yahoo.
Oh it's so iggily wiggily tiggily,
Iggily wiggily tiggily,
Delicious too.
I want some meatballs, meatballs,
    meatballs
And spaghetti.
I'm always ready, to eat spaghet-
    tiiiiiiii.
And that will make me very
    merry.*

Arrangement © Edward G. Kean and
    Robert E. Smith, 1987

Don't laugh. The Flub-a-Dub's passion for meatballs and spaghetti may have paved the way for lasagna's stranglehold on Garfield the Cat. More to the point, our nation's children professed an inexplicable urge to add meatballs and spaghetti to their diets.

I still get thank-you letters from Franco-American.

As I reflect on Doodyville's denizens, it occurs to me that necessity and accident may have spurred the early stage of our creative process more often than not. With Clarabell. With the Flub-a-Dub. With the new, improved Howdy Doody.

The reason it comes to mind is because several other guys sprang up from our anticipation of utter catastrophe. We'd gotten to thinking, what if something ever happened to Howdy? What if he somehow became damaged beyond recognition? (How much publicized plastic surgery can one little fellow endure?) We needed a spare.

We tried and tried, making some huge number of pseudo-Howdys. It turns out there's absolutely no such thing as an exact duplicate when craftsmen handmake, handmold, and sculpt. Even identical twins never look exactly alike. Out of all the Howdys, only one sufficed for the camera, provided we didn't use him for tight shots. We called him Double Doody, and he did the show a few times. He even ran against Howdy for president one year, under the guise of the mysterious Mr. X. As Mr. X, he campaigned for everything kids would hate, such as more homework and shorter summer vacations. Naturally, this unpopular platform strengthened Howdy's chances for victory—which Double Doody later revealed had been his plan all along.

From a distance, Double Doody passed muster just fine. Had we used him in any close-ups, the kids would have recognized instantly that something didn't click. Double Doody now resides in the Smithsonian Institution in Washington, D.C.

Another pseudo-Howdy became Photo Doody, whom we use with the press and media. A Howdy Doody without strings, he has ball socket joints in his wrists, elbows, shoulders, hips, and ankles. Comfortable sitting, standing, shaking hands, and whatever else he might be called upon to do, Photo is a real pro when it comes to picture sessions.

A third almost-Howdy received a Sherlock Holmes–type deerstalker hat and cape and moustache and presto, Inspector John J. Fadoozle, "America's number one—boi-i-i-i-nggg—puh-rivate eye." When we made him, Roger suggested that he get individual eye sockets, which would enable him to wink. Fadoozle claimed, "There's never been a mystery I couldn't solve it." A wink and boi-i-i-i-nngggg noises followed him for emphasis. The boi-i-i-i-nngggg emanated from—what else?—a boinnnng stick, which is the technical term for a long piece of wood with pegs such as those used to tune guitars or violins. The wood protrudes from what for all the world could be a cigar box. A flexible metal string runs along the wood. We'd twist the string taut with the pegs and pluck it, producing the wuh-uh-uh-uh-uhnnng effect.

In due course, the Inspector also ran against Howdy as Mr. X in a presidential campaign.

Then we took *another* pseudo-Howdy, furnishing him with a beard, a cane, and the duds of an old man, and named him Grandpa Doody. Grandpa Doody can best be described as a cross between Howdy Doody and an old geezer. I did his voice—the only voice I ever did on the show besides Howdy's (and Double Doody's all of

Howdy and I pose with Clarabell (Bob Keeshan), Vice President Alben Barkley (left), Senator West (next to Bob), and Attorney General Tom Clark on the steps of the Capitol for "I Am an American Day."

once). Grandpa appeared in a couple of plots, but never developed into a strong character. As a rule, a particular story line would require certain characters. We'd use them, and if we liked them and if they drew a very favorable response, we'd bring them back again and again. But if the character couldn't stand on his own, we didn't force the issue.

After all these false starts to make back-up Howdys, *it* finally happened. Howdy, Bobby Keeshan as Clarabell, and I had been invited to participate in the "I Am an American Day" celebration on the steps of the Capitol in Washington, D.C., with former heavyweight champion Joe Louis. We flew down, had a grand time, and flew back.

I transported Howdy in a special fiberglass case. It looked like a little casket—prophetically, I suppose. I

strapped him, checked him through, and didn't open the box until I got to work. We'd moved him this way before without mishap. And so, wrongly, I assumed he'd be okay once more.

I got what I deserved for assuming. When we took him out Monday in the studio, his head was split in two. Scott Brinker and Bernie Morchen worked feverishly to repair the damage. Scott, in addition to puppets, made many of the props. Bernie, our unit prop manager, had considerable skill with inanimate objects and also with locating live animals on short notice. Together they reglued Howdy, and we did the show without a hitch. But we never did succeed in creating a true duplicate Howdy Doody.

One character who started as a puppet had a whole lot going for her. In fact, everything, except the fact that she was a puppet. We remedied this situation by bringing her to life. She initially happened when Marty Stone observed that all our licensing arrangements revolved around unisex products or products exclusively for boys. Nothing for just girls. We had no female characters on *The Howdy Doody Show* for girls to relate to. All of us, including the Flub-a-Dub, were boys or men.

Acknowledging the oversight, we introduced Princess Summerfall Winterspring of the Tinka Tonka tribe as a puppet. Rhoda Mann did the voice and operated her. This opened a rich vein of licensing possibilities, yet we couldn't help feeling that as a character, the princess lacked life. Howdy, Mr. Bluster, Dilly, and the Flub-a-Dub gave the impression that they could cut their strings, saunter off the stage, and do as they pleased. They had personalities. But I had no more feeling for this princess than I did for Grandpa Doody.

What I said a while ago about Howdy holds true for all of our characters who succeeded as personalities. We never referred to them as puppets. As far as we were concerned, they were people. We never said "Put the camera on the dummy." It would be "Go to Mr. Bluster," or "Camera three to Dilly." It happened often enough that engineers operating the boom mikes would forget that our little guys weren't actually talking; so if I walked away from Howdy after speaking to him, if Howdy was still talking via a recording, the engineer would keep the mike on Howdy and forget to follow me with it. That's how real they seemed.

But the princess puppet was just a puppet. Fortunately, someone noticed singer-dancer Judy Tyler performing locally. She was certainly one of the most beautiful women I've ever seen in person. We auditioned Judy, and after hearing her sing, watching her dance, talking to her, we had no doubts whatsoever. Here was personality beyond our wildest dreams. We hired this wonderful, refreshing, dynamic young lady on the spot.

Eddie Kean came up with the idea for transforming the puppet princess into the real, live Judy on Judy's first *Howdy Doody Show*. The kids adored her at first sight. So did the mothers, the fathers, the grandparents. Girls looked up to her. Boys, who would have several years to go before clapping eyes on Annette Funicello, couldn't get over her. Naturally, Judy became a great favorite and regular on our program. In addition, she and I did public appearances. She danced, and sang charmingly in her own voice. Then, because Judy had an uncanny ear, she could also imitate Ethel Merman, Judy Garland, and other famous songbirds flawlessly. I can't say enough about her. I loved to perform with her, one of the greatest talents we ever had on our show or anybody had on anybody's show. I might add that she was a spectacular, caring, gracious human being.

POPULATING DOODYVILLE

4

DOODYVILLE DISASTERS

Year in, year out, we citizens of Doodyville engaged in one after another fantastic cliffhanger, for instance the adventure of the Mangle Wurzel, or the mystery of the Lucky Left Leg of a Lima Llama. But not all our cliffhangers occurred on camera.

For the Peanuts in the gallery, the biggest cliffhanger had invariably been whether they would get tickets of admission. We had forty seats in the Peanut Gallery each day, and two sponsors each day. Each of the day's sponsors received ten tickets. I got four each day; each actor had four a week. The rest went to the affiliates, to station relations, and to the relatives of network executives. We got thousands of mail-in requests for tick-

ets yet could fill very, very few. For a while, we tried to sneak in a dozen more kids each afternoon, by seating them on the floor in front of the Peanut Gallery. It came to the point that we had as many "sneakers" as we did ticket holders. When the fire department learned of this, they yelled "fire hazard" and assigned a fireman to the studio every day to enforce a strict ceiling of forty Peanuts.

One little boy who entered the magic circle has since been immortalized by a poem. During a Halloween show, while I narrated an old-time movie, the youngster fastened himself on my arm and pant leg, chattering at me as I talked to the camera. I sat up on the Peanut Gallery ledge with the forty kids, and we all watched the film on the monitor. The only other person in the immediate vicinity was the organist, playing background music. The rest of the crew stood off in the distance.

There was a sleepy character in the movie. I nicknamed him Rip Van Winkle. But the little boy ignored this in favor of his own conversation. A few of his words finally penetrated my efforts at concentration. He whispered to me, "Buffalo Bob! Buffalo Bobbb! I gotta tinkle!" Obviously I couldn't go tinkling with him, so I pointed to several stage hands and cameramen, thinking he'd walk over to them and find a tinkle partner. Unfortunately, in the same direction as I had indicated, we had a tremendous lighted pumpkin on the floor. He must have thought I meant the pumpkin, because he went over and . . . put out the candle.

The camera crew saw him first and howled. I didn't see it. I had my eyes glued to the monitor. The Pea-

nuts, hearing the camera crew, looked around for the source of the merriment. Then they not only laughed but squealed, as kids do. Through their cacophony of noises, I made out "Buffalo Bob! Buffalo Bob! Sissy in the pumpkin!" I turned, expecting to see some minor distraction, and fell apart. I collapsed into hysterics—as I do—bent over, and couldn't catch my breath. Dayton Allen climbed down from the puppet bridge, concluded the narration, did the commercial and closed the show, while I crawled off on my hands and knees.

Following the program, we got phone calls and letters from the audience in TV-land who hadn't a clue what was funny. They'd been watching an old-time movie, nothing at all to laugh at, when suddenly everyone was hysterical. The movie was over. Buffalo Bob was gone. And they wanted to know what was such a panic on *The Howdy Doody Show*. Mil and I came up with a poem that was sent to everyone who had raised the question:

The Peanut Gallery on our special Father's Day Show, June 1949, includes famous fathers Bennett Cerf (upper left), moderator John K. M. McCaffrey (second dad from upper left), Tex McCrary (upper right), Paul Winchell with his dummy, Jerry Mahoney (bottom center), Morey Amsterdam (second from lower right), and Andre Baruch (lower right).

So many of you asked what hap-
*   pened*
On the night of Hallowe'en
When everyone was hysterical
And Buffalo Bob had to leave the
*   scene.*
It was during an old-time movie
About a man named Rip Van
*   Winkle,*
When a four-year-old boy from the
*   Gallery*
Told Bob that he had to tinkle.
Well, Buffalo Bob couldn't take
*   him,*
So he pointed to someone who
*   could.*
But the little kid didn't follow di-
*   rections,*
He just walked to a pumpkin and
*   stood.*
Well, the rest of the story is ob-
*   vious*
And we didn't even need a mop.
'Cause our little friend had great
*   aim*
And he never spilled a drop.

Considering its role in history, the pumpkin constituted a remarkably uncomplicated prop. Others had greater refinements—and ramifications. The Scoopdoodle, a monitor with crazy gadgets affixed to it, tuned in our old-time movies. The Super Talk-O-Scope could dial in anybody, anytime, anywhere. If Howdy or I went on a mission, the cameraman would dolly into the Super Talk-O-Scope and there we would be, saying our say.

The Flapdoodle, shaped like a pipe about a foot in diameter, gave people whatever they wanted, as long as they wanted something good. Couldn't be bad. Had to be good. It worked by virtue of a prop man backstage thrusting the requested object through the pipe on a stick. We'd request something good, open the trap on the Flapdoodle, and son of a gun, there it was.

The Electromindomizer, which read minds, employed an antihistamine tube, a cathode glass tube, and a sink generator. We'd use it to penetrate characters' thought processes. Bluster tried to get it away from us, providing about two months' worth of cliffhangers for the show. I remember being on Edward R. Murrow's *Person to Person* during this period. When he signed off, the esteemed TV journalist's closing words were "And incidentally, Bob, when you're through with the Electromindomizer, do you mind if I use it?"

The Honkadoodle translated Mother Goose, an old stuffed goose who answered our questions in goose talk. We'd put her bill up to the microphone. She'd "gwak gawk honwdwkkw." Then we'd tear a typewritten sheet of paper from the Honkadoodle, read it, and divulge her message. You can understand how this would be a valuable tool to have.

The Mangle Wurzel, a hex, consisted of a Brillo pad stuck on cardboard. When superimposed over a

Edward R. Murrow and I discuss what we'll be talking about on Person to Person, *May 1954.*

character's head, it caused the character to behave irrationally—to dance funny, or act like a chicken, or whatever. Mr. Bluster controlled the Mangle Wurzel. Before long, we heard from parents that children wouldn't sleep at night for fear Mr. Bluster lurked in the bushes, ready to Mangle Wurzel them.

"Mommy, I won't have a Mangle Wurzel over my head tonight, will I?"

"No, Junior, go to sleep. I checked the closets, I checked under the bed. No Mangle Wurzels here."

We dropped the Mangle Wurzel, perhaps recycling it to scrub a pot.

The Three Flying Gonkletwerps, like the Mangle Wurzel, petrified kids. How were we to know? In their favor, the Gonkletwerps were a budget bonanza, because they were invisible. Howdy would enthuse, "There they go, Buffalo Bob! They're by the trees!" Children across America broke out

into a cold sweat. The switchboards lit up with more parents calling: "Now you've got our Junior hiding from something he can't even see." Eddie thought he had the answer: "Let's rename them the Three Friendly Invisible Gonkletwerps." But we still bombed.

"Mommy, I'm afraid to sleep. The Gonkletwerps are in my room."

"Don't worry. I checked the closets. I checked under the bed. No Gonkletwerps."

"Well, of course you didn't see them. They're invisible. And they're gonna get me!!!"

In the course of another saga concerning a series of animals and objects whose names began with the letter *L*, a lamb—actually, a big, smelly sheep—left an organic surprise on stage. The puppeteers up on the puppet bridge saw it first. Dayton laughed so hard he had difficulty delivering his

DOODYVILLE DISASTERS —————

lines. I got wind of it before seeing this big job on the toe of my boot. I kicked it offstage, then sensed a giggle fit coming on. I walked offstage after it, calling over my shoulder "Mr. Bluster, you're so smart. You take over." I knew Dayton, manipulating Bluster, could ad-lib his way out of anything. As I stood out of camera range chuckling, I noticed stage hands walking around the dung rather than removing it. The crew refused to take a position on who should scoop it up. TV unions, as yet in their formative stages, had still to address such issues. Sizing up the situation—they were union, I was a guy in a pith helmet and riding pants—I went back out and cleaned it up myself.

This particular adventure unfolded over several months. We had a Mystery of the Five L's. Was it a Lucky Left Leg? Lucky Left Leg of a what? Of a Lamb? Fortunately, no. It turned out to be the Lucky Left Leg of the Lima Llama. But to Mil, the denouement is anticlimactic. She fondly remembers the experience as "Bob's brush with Plop Art."

About a week before the 1952 elections, Kellogg's had a gigantic convention in New Orleans. They invited Clarabell, Princess Summerfall Winterspring, Marty Stone, and me to appear and entertain. Prerecording shows and segments before we left, we happily headed for the Crescent City. Every night we saw the bands, the acts, the best that Bourbon Street had

to offer. One—Zippy the Chimpanzee—knocked our socks off. Zippy perched himself on a highchair, fed himself cereal, and applauded himself. On the cue word *think*, he gave a raspberry.

"Zippy, what do you think of the election?"

"Phthphoooofffff!"

Eager to whisk Zippy to Doodyville, we approached his trainer, Lee Ecuyer. Lee said, "Okay, but he works with Bonnie."

"What do you mean?"

"My wife."

"What does she do?"

"She strips."

"Uh, what exactly would a stripper do on *The Howdy Doody Show*?" We bargained, arriving at a price that justified Bonnie's keeping her clothes on. Then Eddie Kean had to write for Zippy, which he contends is one of the hardest chores he ever, ever took on. It couldn't go on forever. How much mileage could we expect from a chimp who knew a few tricks and how to spit? Poor Eddie.

Zippy surprised us, though, with an unexpected stunt. He hated Mr. Bluster. We deduced that it had to be the voice. As a result, whenever Zippy saw Bluster, he ran over and throttled or smacked him, practically separating him from his marionette strings. Zippy also despised water, as apparently all chimps do—maybe because they sense that the crocodiles get the slow ones. We discovered this when we tried an appearance with Zippy at the Bonnie Briar Country Club in Larchmont. It was supposed to be poolside, but as soon as Zippy neared the pool, he hid in the car. We couldn't coax him out. He just cried and screamed and cried.

Be that as it may, I understand we pioneered this phenomenon of anthropomorphic TV, long before J. Fred Muggs scored his triumph as a regular on Dave Garroway's *Today* show. Ah, the challenge of nascent television! We were all such masochists then.

One of our liveliest disasters befell in the last weeks of 1952. On camera, kids saw only the amazing conclusion of another of our cliffhangers. Former Peanut David White—who remembers Doodyville about as well as his hometown—has re-created, *from memory*, the events leading up to that fateful finale:

"I began watching *The Howdy Doody Show* in earnest the week before Easter, 1952. That was the week that Mr. Bluster went off to Mexico to meet Mr. X. The inspector followed. On the Friday before Easter, Bluster was seen, via the Super Talk-O-Scope, in a cave speaking to Mr. X, who was not on camera. In a previous scene, the inspector was outside the cave waiting for Bluster and Mr. X to come out. Before Mr. X was revealed, the Super Talk-O-Scope blew out a picture tube and we were left hanging. Princess Summerfall Winterspring sang

'Easter Parade.' By Monday the Super Talk-O-Scope was repaired and Mexico was tuned in again. By this time the Inspector was still outside the cave, but the cave was empty. Bluster and Mr. X had gone out another entrance.

"The rest of the spring, summer, and early fall was built around Mr. X's identity. Mr. Bluster's English brother Hector Hamhock seemed a likely candidate, as did Chief Thunderthud. A sky hopper was another possibility. In June Buffalo Bob received a letter from Big Ben, the owner of the circus, informing everybody that the circus would be torn down to make way for a gravel dump, but that Howdy and his friends would be able to move to a new clubhouse. Mr. Bluster had been trying to take over the circus for some time, and without telling him the circus would be torn down, Howdy handed it over to Bluster. For two days Bluster reigned supreme and called the show *The Mr. X Show.* On Friday, June 20, in came the wreckers who demolished the circus, much to Bluster's dismay. By Monday the gang was in the new clubhouse and Bluster was scheming to get four rooms for himself. I was away for the summer and unable to follow the show until September.

"I returned just in time for the revelation of Mr. X's identity. It was explained that Mr. X was locked up in a tree. Bluster, Dilly Dally, and Thunderthud stalled for time. Finally Thunderthud unlocked the tree and Mr. X walked out on the puppet stage, wearing a square 'caboose' around him marked 'I am Mr. X.' For three days his identity remained a mystery and he communicated only by mechanical noises. Howdy ventured a guess that Mr. X was John J. Fadoozle. The princess consulted her magic power necklace and confirmed that it was indeed John J..

"The name didn't mean anything at that time. Finally Clarabell tore apart the 'caboose' and unveiled Mr. X. The inspector! The inspector admitted that from now on he *was* John J. Fadoozle, America's number-one (boing!)

private eye! Obviously, the inspector had become impatient waiting outside the cave in Mexico and had gone to find Mr. Bluster.

"The rest of 1952 was spent preparing for the election. I remember voting on a ballot off a loaf of Wonder Bread, for Howdy, of course, and sending it in. The princess consulted her magic necklace and was told that Buffalo Bob should stay near the ballots so that Bluster would not steal Howdy's votes. The necklace was stolen by an evil magician, and a week

was spent trying to track it down in a magic forest. Thunderthud found it, but it wouldn't obey him. Finally the princess retrieved it. Two days before the election, Thunderthud found all of Howdy's votes and carried them out of town. Buffalo Bob was in hot pursuit. Judge Sir Archibald counted the ballots, with Mr. X in the lead. Howdy recruited Flub-a-Dub Jr.—the Flub-a-Dub's son—to rescue the ballots, and Howdy achieved a landslide victory.

"The day after the election, November 5, 1952, was the day that Nick Nicholson made his debut as J. Cornelius Cobb. The J. stood for Jasper. From the first, Cobb indicated that he did not like clowns. Then followed Clarabell's initiation into the Ooragnak tribe, while Thunderthud tried everything to prevent Clarabell from becoming an Indian. Buffalo Bob rescued Clarabell when he discovered that if anyone was absent from Doodyville for more than ten days, he would not be allowed back in town. So Clarabell returned in the nick of time.

"A Chicapoodle—combination of chicken and poodle on a puppet string—flew into town. Bluster captured it and found written on its tag that there was a substantial reward for its rescue. Bluster and Dilly Dally set off to find the owner, Lulie Belle Widgeon.

"Just before Christmas, Bargain Bill appeared and tricked Clarabell into trading a six-leaf clover for a horse. The horse ran away with Clarabell, as Bobby Keeshan exited."

I'd call that thrilling stuff. Kids hung on our every word and drove parents crazy if they had to miss an episode. If it's any consolation, we suffered horribly behind-the-scenes over this one.

The trouble began when Bobby Keeshan, Dayton Allen, and Bill LeCornec got a raise. They'd been getting scale, which I believe amounted to $375 a week. When it came to the end of each week, the person making out the payroll would ask, "What commercial was who in and how much extra do they get?" I believe Roger Muir said, "Wouldn't it be easier just to double their salaries and avoid this nickel-and-diming?"

There's another of those stupid rumors afoot that I didn't want anyone else doing commercials, because I preferred to keep the income to myself. No way, Don José. I received my regular salary, considerably more than scale, therefore I didn't get another cent for commercials. I appreciated the relief when another actor did one and had absolutely no objection to my friends getting the money.

When Roger suggested doubling their salaries, I loved the idea. They deserved the raises. I was pleased that we had the means to make what was undeniably a very attractive arrangement for Bobby, Dayton, and Bill. Then, as I understand it, Bobby found

Howdy, Dilly Dally, the Flub-a-Dub, and Mr. Bluster witness a typical Doodyville debate—which Clarabell (Bob Keeshan) is about to settle with seltzer.

an agent. The agent contacted Roger Muir, advising Roger that he represented all three men plus Rhoda Mann, Howdy's puppeteer, and that they each demanded $1,000 a week or they would quit. I should add that Rhoda didn't receive any $750 a week because in those days, many good puppeteers could be hired for $100 a week.

When this agent threatened his all-or-nothing deal—take all four for $4,000 a week or all four walk—he indulged in what is called collective bargaining, and as such is against AFTRA rules. Performers are not allowed to bargain collectively. Any one of them could have gone to Roger and made an ultimatum for $10,000 a week, but two or more is a different matter entirely. It becomes not a question of negotiation but of ransom. NBC informed Roger that he simply could not entertain the discussion on those terms. Roger thereupon went to

each one separately, trying to reason with them: "You're destroying yourselves. Come to me individually. Make the deal for yourself. Please." They didn't.

Roger told the agent that it wouldn't be possible. Maybe one or two *could* have gotten a raise individually. One or two had tremendous talent, did voices, worked puppets, and appeared on stage. But all four? One of whom was Rhoda? Roger and Marty and Eddie and I discussed our options, hating to lose some of them, yet we couldn't escape the truth. They left us no choice. They left it at an ultimatum: Pay us or we walk. As Yogi Berra once said, it was *déjà vu* all over again. I was waiting for Frank Paris to show up and carry them off in his little cloth bag.

On the day we had to make our decision, I asked for everybody to be in the studio fifteen minutes earlier.

HOWDY AND ME

By everybody, I mean the cameramen, lighting men, engineers, production people, cast, everyone. When they had assembled, I said, "We're going to have some personnel changes here on *The Howdy Doody Show*. You're going to hear a million different stories about what happened, so I want to tell you right now, all of you, what has been going on. And I want to tell it in front of Bobby Keeshan, Dayton Allen, Bill LeCornec, and Rhoda Mann. This is what happened, and if I make any statement incorrectly, I want them to correct me now, or else this will be it, the accepted truth." And I told them the story.

I explained that three had been getting scale, then double scale. I continued, "Bobby Keeshan contacted an agent, who contacted Roger. They gave Roger an ultimatum, stating that Bobby, Dayton, Bill, and Rhoda would have to get $1,000 a week or they're going to quit. I want you to know, they have made their decision. They are quitting *The Howdy Doody Show* as of now. Good luck, Bobby, Dayton, Bill, Rhoda. Now, come on, gang, we've got a lot of work to do."

That was how I "fired" those four in what has since so ridiculously been referred to as the "Christmas Eve Massacre." Aside from the fact that I couldn't have fired them—inasmuch as their employer was NBC, not Bob Smith—I find it fascinating that professionals would jeopardize a series so close to the holidays, fully aware of the gamble they took with their own livelihoods, and then somehow cast themselves as the victims of a "massacre" because their intended victims managed to survive beautifully for at least another eight years on network television.

Bobby Keeshan went on to work for his father-in-law as a mortician. Dayton got a regular role on Steve Allen's show, gaining particular visibility for his portrayal in the "Man in the Street" interview as the guy with the catchline "Why not?" Dayton returned to our show for the tenth anniversary. He's still a good friend, fun to work with and a riot to relax with. Bill departed, but not for long. We missed him and needed him, and were thrilled when he accepted our invitation to rejoin the family soon after.

Maybe three or four years after the "massacre" incident, Rhoda Mann sued the National Broadcasting Company, contending that she hadn't received scale when the other actors did. But the AFTRA rules never covered puppeteers per se. NBC and Rhoda met in a court of arbitration. I appeared as a witness and, not wanting to perjure myself, conceded that I could not in fairness compare her talent to Dayton's or Bill's. She never even did Howdy's voice. I did. She just pulled Howdy's strings. She argued that it's tough to make a puppet look sad and happy when he has the same face all the time. But that's what puppeteers do, what they're paid for.

Some version of the story has it that I begged Rhoda to come back three times. I never asked her to come back, not even once. I believe that NBC settled her suit for some small remuneration, perhaps a few thousand dollars. But I never saw her again.

I'd be surprised to hear that anyone in the audience noticed the slightest change in Howdy after Rhoda Mann left, making her departure, at best, incidental. Bobby Keeshan's exit is another matter, because after all, he went on to become Captain Kangaroo—a sort of incipient Mister Rogers—for a whole generation of youngsters.

Last year when Bobby did *The Pat Sajak Show*, he recorded a brief videotape to be run in connection with my appearance on Pat's program a few weeks later. In it, he said of me, "He taught me my craft. He taught me about timing. He taught me about comedy. If Bob didn't do all of these things, the Captain would never have been. So Father Bob, thanks a lot."

I'm proud that Howdy and I gave him his start on television, and grateful for Bobby's assistance in any number of ways, especially during our early years together. I've publicly praised him, and he's publicly praised me. If he'd been willing to let it rest on this note of mutual admiration, I'd have been pleased and in fact relieved to go along. But as long as he chose to expand on his feelings in his book, *Growing Up Happy*, I'd be remiss not to concede that our memories differ on fundamental points, including the conclusion of his Doodyville tenure. I'll add that I called him "Bobby" rather than "Bob," motivated by affection and camaraderie and not, as he suggested, to label him with a "childish diminutive." It's not as if I called him Booby, and when people speak of Bobby Kennedy, Bobby Thompson, or Bobby Sarnoff, it doesn't seem to me that they do it with any disrespect. For the record, we had six Bobs on Howdy's set—Bob Keeshan, Bob Nicholson, Bob Hultgren, Bob Rippen, Bob Hopkins, and Bob Smith. Consequently, whenever someone yelled "Bob!" six of us came running. At one point we decided to streamline communications by referring to Keeshan as "Bobby," Nicholson as "Nick," Hultgren as "Bob," Rippen as "Rip," Hopkins as "Hoppy," and Smith as "the Buff." That's the story, plain and simple. Bob(by) Keeshan has, however, correctly noted that we would have wished him to have a greater range of talent.

We tried to teach him a musical instrument, to get him to play even a few notes on the xylophone. No luck. It became a sore point with us that we paid him so much to do so little. Granted, the kids loved Clarabell with the seltzer and the horns and the slapstick. I won't underrate his contributions. But if he couldn't play any horns more complex than the two on his clown box, surely we were entitled to add a Clarabell to our cast who could.

We called AFTRA, asked for someone with talent, and were delighted to learn of the availability of Gil Lamb, a fine eccentric dancer. Eddie Kean, relishing the idea, tackled the on-camera transition to Gil, tall and thin, from Bobby, who was neither. He devised the Clownstretcher. Beginning with a stand-in Keeshan's size, we ran Clarabell through this Clownstretcher. Presto! A larger Clarabell stepped out.

Parents raised flack: "Who are you kidding? This isn't the real Clarabell." Ironically, through no fault of his own, Gil didn't last. During a rehearsal, while dancing a fancy, energetic routine, he tripped and hit his chest on the arm of a chair. His whole weight landed on the arm, breaking several of his ribs, and I've never seen anybody writhe in pain as much as he did. Unable to wait out his recovery, we had to enlist a new clown.

We'd already sent to Buffalo for Nick Nicholson, who had as much talent as anybody I'd ever known in the industry. Nick, you'll recall, used to perform with me in Buffalo. He sang and played great trombone, string bass, piano, organ, and was a marvelous arranger. Mil and I invited him and his wife, Janie, to our home in Pound Ridge for the weekend. (Our Pound Ridge home, which began as a weekend hideaway, developed into quite a spread over the years. Marty had the adjoining property.)

Nick, Marty, and I adjourned to the basement to confirm what Nick could do and what *The Howdy Doody Show* could do with it. Nick so impressed Marty that we persuaded Roger to let us invent another character. Nick became J. Cornelius Cobb, who ran the general store and wore many hats. He'd have a fireman's hat and be the fireman, a policeman's hat and be the policeman, and so on.

Nick recalls a little friction when he first arrived on the scene: "Bobby Keeshan, backstage, informed me that I'd be packed off to Buffalo in no time." To the contrary, Nick had been with us for a little under two months when Clarabell traded the six-leaf clover for a horse and rode off on it into the sunset.

On camera, we had to deal with the mass retreat of Clarabell, Thunderthud, Mr. Bluster, Dilly Dally, and company. How? I searched for them via the Super Talk-O-Scope, determining that Bluster had been shipwrecked on the appropriately named Changing Island in the Gulf of Mexico. His brothers went to rescue him, to no avail. Clarabell had lost the horse but found a diver's helmet and swam to Changing Island. I flew there in the Aerodoodle to meet them. Then came a commotion: Somebody's in a diver's helmet in the harbor. We fished the stranger from the harbor, opened the helmet, and introduced the face of Nick Nicholson as Clarabell for the first time. Eddie Kean had wanted this

approach to avoid scaring the children—and provoking the parents—with another dramatic transformation à la the Clownstretcher. Even Changing Island had its relatively normal days once in a while.

We continued to add characters. With Rhoda Mann's departure, we piped a new puppeteer aboard—Rufus Rose—who assumed Howdy duty. In short order, Rufus also introduced such cute animal puppets as the bears Hyde and Zeke and Tiz the Dinosaur (with a voice somewhere between Sir Archibald's and Eleanor Roosevelt's). Among other puppeteers we had Rufus's wife, Margo, and Lee Carney and her husband, Mike King. They excelled, though I'd be negligent not to mention that at one time or another, everybody on the show operated a marionette—except me, who was generally on the floor talking to the characters. Not that they all did it well. But when we had seven or eight figures out there at once, everybody had to climb on the bridge and pull strings, including our three Clarabells—Bobby Keeshan, Nick Nicholson, and Lew Anderson.

During the spring Mr. Bluster (now voiced by Allen Swift, who also did Flub-a-Dub's) sported with Miss Lulie Belle Widgeon, tricked me into leaving Doodyville on a spaceship, and announced the commencement of his own *The Howdy Bluster Show*. For this, Lee Carney manipulated marionettes and also created the live role of Mr. Bluster's Aunt Hazel. Allen Swift, meanwhile, donned feathers to portray Chief Thunderchicken—a rival to Bill LeCornec's Chief Thunderthud who had rejoined the fold. Nick Nicholson had done Dilly Dally's voice, but Bill assumed that responsibility when he returned, as well as reprising Oil Well Willie, Doctor Singasong, and his repertoire of live characters.

When other shows picked up on Judy Tyler's talent, she requested a leave of absence. In October of 1953 we promoted Princess Summerfall Winterspring to Queen Mother of the Tinka Tonka tribe, thus facilitating her departure from *The Howdy Doody Show*. From Doodyville, she went on to such impressive prime-time programs as *The Milton Berle Show* and *The Colgate Comedy Hour*, and on to Broadway in Rodgers and Hammerstein's *Pipe Dream*. Her big break came with a role as Elvis Presley's love interest in the 1957 movie *Jailhouse Rock*. Many critics consider it the only one of his thirty-one pictures to capture his electricity. It cinched the King's reputation as a singing James Dean, meanwhile launching our princess on the path to major stardom. Hot on the heels of its success, Judy signed a multipicture deal.

Judy fell in love for real on the West Coast, married there, then headed East with her new husband. They never arrived. An automobile accident ended their lives in Billy the

---

🖅 *Clarabell (Nick Nicholson) and I help light the tree at Rockefeller Center, 1953.*

Kid, Wyoming, on July 4, 1957. I can
only imagine the career she would
have enjoyed had she survived. Her
sensational sparkle could have lighted
up the world for so many years to
come.

Rufus Rose,
with Captain Scuttlebutt,
Howdy, and Dilly Dally.

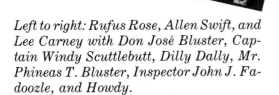

Left to right: Rufus Rose, Allen Swift, and
Lee Carney with Don José Bluster, Cap-
tain Windy Scuttlebutt, Dilly Dally, Mr.
Phineas T. Bluster, Inspector John J. Fa-
doozle, and Howdy.

5

THE BEAT GOES ON

*D*isasters notwithstanding, the early Fifties were Howdy's boom years. In allocating commercial minutes, networks had *A*, *B*, and *C* designations. For *A*, prime time, they charged 100 percent of the going advertising rate. For *C*, daytime, they got 50 percent. *B* time, halfway between *A* and *C*, commanded 75 percent. *The Howdy Doody Show* became NBC's first *B* offering. Yet with our six minutes of commercials per day and five half-hour shows a week, NBC realized greater income from *Howdy* than they did from their prime-time ratings grabbers, which ran only an hour a week. On the strength of its commercials alone, *The Howdy Doody Show* was NBC's leading money-maker.

That was just in terms of what sponsors paid for on-air commercials. In addition, there were Howdy-related promotions and tie-ins. Continental Baking paid us $100,000 a year for the use of the Howdy Doody characters who appeared on the end seals of loaves of Wonder Bread. The year 1950 alone saw $15 million generated from Howdy-licensed items. Sponsorship and licensing prospered, geometrically, as if it would never end. It brought cute misunderstandings, as when Kate, the little daughter of some of our dearest friends, Dr. Fred and Margaret McLellan, came downstairs carrying a big box with her beautiful new party frock in it. Her mother asked, "Honey, what's this for?"

Kate answered, "I want to win

Buffalo Bob's contest for the wading pool, and he said on *The Howdy Doody Show* that to win, we have to send him our name and a dress."

Along with cute misunderstandings, sponsorship and licensing provided a springboard for some full-fledged fiascos.

One brainstorm—hardly my favorite memory—involved Welch's Grape Juice and milk. Some clever advertising person, in an effort to differentiate the tasty grape juice from soda pop, decided that the popularity and importance of milk, the number-one drink of children, could be used to elevate grape juice to an uncontested number-two position. We hoped to achieve this, and do kids a huge favor, by persuading them of the virtues of combining the two in a "royal purple cow." Welch's circulated story booklets in the supermarkets about a cow who crept into a grape arbor and ate enough grapes to turn purple; when she gave milk, all the boys and girls proclaimed it the finest they ever tasted.

Finally Howdy, Clarabell, and I made a public appearance to unveil the Royal Purple Cow at a huge shopping

Bill LeCornec as Chief Thunderthud (left), Lee Carney (background), Clarabell (Nick Nicholson), Allen Swift (Chief Thunderchicken, background), and I help Howdy put his hand prints in wet cement at Grauman's Chinese Theatre, January 1954.

DONNA: When Buffalo Bob sold products, kids listened. What do you think about the flack that sort of thing gets today?
BOB: We didn't sell them products that parents would object to. We sold toothpaste, and got them to brush after each meal; breakfast cereal, which got them to eat breakfast; enriched bread, which made them aware of vitamins and minerals; and juice, which lured them away from soft drinks.

center in New Jersey. The cow had been dyed purple with extreme care and every precaution for its safety. As an outward proof of our concern, we had humane society representatives, veterinarians, and nurses accompanying us on the platform. One by one we introduced them; so that one by one they left the cow waiting behind a curtain on the platform. When everyone had abandoned the cow, she grew bored, or restless, or whatever would cause a cow to break loose and saunter off the platform. This saunter resulted in an eight-foot drop. The Royal Purple Cow crashed into the hard ground, shattering her leg, bellowing in pain. The vets, nurses, and humane society representatives ran to her aid, leaving me on the platform alone. "Gee, folks, I—" The Royal Purple Cow drowned me out with her deafening screams. A truck drove up to take her away. The cow couldn't be treated and had to be

THE BEAT GOES ON —————————

shot. We didn't convince many people to drink grape juice laced with milk that day.

Later Eddie Kean told us, "If you really want to differentiate Welch's from soda pop, I've got the perfect slogan for you: 'Welch's squelches belches.'"

We headed off another potential defeat, diverting it into a minor symbolic victory. Our sponsor, Colgate's, had instructed us to sing and play their jingle until every child in America knew it as well as the national anthem. As far as I can tell, we soon had every tot and toddler committing our ditty to heart.

Brush your teeth with Colgate's,
Colgate Dental Cream.
It cleans your breath
(Wotta toothpaste)
While it cleans your teeth.
(Colgate toothpaste.)
Cleans your breath.
(Wotta toothpaste)
And it tastes so good.

Reprinted by permission of the Colgate-Palmolive Company

One evening on the six twenty-five train going from Grand Central Station to Larchmont, a man from Colgate's relaxed smugly, reading his newspaper. Next to him sat an account executive from Ipana toothpaste. The Ipana man said to the Colgate's man, "You know something? I was never so insulted. Last night my little two-

DONNA: But you pioneered the use of TV to sell to children.
BOB: I didn't invent it. We simply continued what radio had been doing. What we couldn't have done then is what public TV does now. Back then, sponsors simply didn't pay to produce educational series for children. On the other hand, the more the sponsors paid us, the more we had available for quality productions.

year-old daughter told me she wanted Colgate's, Howdy Doody's toothpaste."

"Well, I certainly hope you were a sport and bought her a tube."

"I did not. I just gave her a tube of Ipana and told her it was Colgate's. She can't read. She doesn't know the difference, and she brushes with it."

The Colgate's man rushed the sad tale to us. "What do we do? We've got a tremendously successful campaign. Only trouble is, it sells toothpaste interchangeably." So we revised our lyrics, and started to sing:

Brush your teeth with Colgate's,
Colgate Dental Cream.
You'll know it's right
If it's red and white.

Reprinted by permission of the Colgate-Palmolive Company

Ipana, in its red and orange tube, was doomed. A week later, the Ipana man bumped into the Colgate man on the

HOWDY AND ME

Howdy and I and an example of a Howdy Doody tie-in product.

six twenty-five. Glaring daggers, he muttered, "You stinker." Perhaps if we represented Ipana instead of Colgate's, Ipana would still be in the stores. Maybe not. Nothing rhymes with orange.

When I did a Tootsie Roll commercial sitting among the Peanuts in the gallery, a little boy began bellowing at me from three rows back. "Buffalo Bob! BUFFALLLO BOBBBBB!" I had no choice but to leave the gallery with the boom mike following after me

and my Tootsie Roll. When I finished, I returned to the bouncing bundle of lung power. "What is it, son?"

"I can't eat Tootsie Rolls. My mother says I'm allergic to chocolate." Though the microphone was off, I had a sinking feeling that we'd lost a sponsor. After the show, the account executive sought me out. "Oh, Bob!"

"Uh-oh."

"You know the little boy who can't eat Tootsie Rolls?"

"Gosh, I'm sorry about that."

THE BEAT GOES ON —————————————

"Don't be. The kid probably isn't allergic. His mother's probably just too cheap to buy him Tootsies."

Sponsors sometimes wanted to break the rules for dramatic effect. I remember some young writer in Ovaltine's advertising agency came up with the brilliant idea that it would be the most impressive thing in the world if Clarabell, who never talked on television, would utter *Ovaltine* as his first word. Wouldn't that be great? But of course we wouldn't do it. For one thing, the other sponsors would have strung us up alive for showing such preferential treatment. For another, think about how unfair that would have been to the kids.

We never, ever tried to con kids. We never took unfair advantage. We never sold a product that could hurt a child. At the very worst, we sold candies—not the best substance to apply to tooth enamel—but because we urged children to brush their teeth, we kept even candy in a balanced perspective. We avoided violence in our stories and our commercials. The only thing ever shot from a gun would be an occasional sponsor's cereal or cookie, but more often than not, we limited our lethal weapons to Clarabell's seltzer bottle. We aimed for parental approval. If the parents had ever stopped respecting our sincerity, we would have lost respect for ourselves.

But within those guidelines, we definitely did right by our sponsors. When I held up a Hostess cupcake,

Ed Wynn, Flub-a-Dub, and Howdy encourage kids to support C.A.R.E.

indicating its luscious cream filling with my pointer, the audience didn't know that an account executive had precut it, scooped out cake, and loaded it with the cream from another three cupcakes. Such practices weren't forbidden yet by the FCC, and we thought them totally ethical and reasonable.

And the money continued to roll in. I mention this by way of leading up to the fact that I didn't see nearly as much of it as might be assumed. In those days, because income tax ran to 92 percent in the higher brackets, a

HOWDY AND ME

number of show-biz moguls hatched the concept of selling individual entertainment entities outright, rendering the proceeds not "income" but rather major capital gains to be taxed at a much lower rate, I think 25 percent. Jack Benny tried it—selling CBS the package of a quirky tightwad with a vault, a Maxwell, and so on—and got dismal results. In his case, the IRS ruled that he couldn't sell the concept of a Jack Benny because it wasn't a tangible property. Yet Freeman F. Gosden and Charles J. Correll, creators and portrayers of *Amos 'n' Andy*, swung the deal nicely by selling their created, copyrighted property and characters. On radio, they'd done the voices. On TV, other actors filled the roles—which couldn't have happened in Jack Benny's instance.

Marty suggested that I go the same route. By selling the Doodyville characters, I'd realize a larger net from an essentially comparable cash flow. When my contract was due to expire in 1950, we went to CBS program chief, Hubbell Robinson. We offered Howdy Doody to CBS. CBS expressed monumental interest and asked to see our contracts. Recognizing from the contracts that NBC had first refusal, CBS said, "What's the point of our making a deal? Whatever we offer, NBC will match it. So what are we doing, other than establishing par for the value of the property? If you can get out of the exclusivity arrangement and deliver your charac-ters unencumbered, we'll be happy to discuss it."

Marty and I pondered, taking our thoughts to Niles Trammell. What we thought was that some network ought to wave a million dollars under our noses. We proposed this to Niles, who replied, "It's a great property, one of the most lucrative I've ever known. So we give you a million dollars. Then what? You go to Cuba or England and we've got the Howdy Doody property, but without you. Come back next week. We'll have a counterproposal."

Marty felt very strongly that we wanted to close the deal before the end of the year, before the tax laws changed. After the Jack Benny and *Amos 'n' Andy* bouts, the IRS planned to abolish capital gains for television programs, books to movies, and the like. Therefore, when Niles presented his figures, we were inclined to listen carefully.

The deal was this: We entered into a capital gains arrangement, selling the properties to Kagran, a corporation formed by NBC and the Lehman Brothers, the big banking concern in New York, to license them. Kagran paid $350,000, half to Marty, half to me. They gave me an additional $250,000 in ten-year debenture bonds, which in fact they would redeem as soon as they cleared the necessary profit. The bonds would pay 3 percent interest—$7,500 annually. The $175,000 cash, plus ten years of interest at $7,500 annually, plus $250,000

Howdy in an international frame of mind, as a Royal Canadian Mountie . . .

worth of bonds, added up to my half million. Marty put up *Author Meets the Critics*, his defunct *Americana* program, and his contracts to handle and manage Gabby Hayes, Peewee Reese, and Jackie Robinson. If memory serves, he threw in the lease to his 58th Street office and his office furniture. In exchange, he received $175,000 cash, 30 percent or 40 percent of Kagran's common stock, and a key position running the operation, licensing Howdy. This gave Marty major incentive to make Kagran profitable—because the more Kagran made, the more his common stock shares would be worth. However, because I had debenture bonds, I'd see money before any stockholders did.

New contracts were drawn between NBC and me as of January 1951. As of January 1, 1951, NBC owned every facet of Howdy Doody—puppets, names, trademarks, licenses—every man, woman, and child in Doodyville with the exception of the name, costume, character, and likeness of Buffalo Bob. At the time, I made $3,500 per week, and with escalator clauses, this would probably have increased to $9,000 or $10,000 per week in ten years. Marty, however, convinced me that I would be crazy to accept $3,500 a week as income, when I could opt for $1,500 cash and $2,000 paid into Kagran for the use of the characters. The more Kagran made, the sooner they'd be able to redeem my $250,000 in debenture bonds. To sweeten the pot, Marty voided the contract that earned him 10 percent of my income. This was the dumbest deal I ever made in my life. How I was talked into this, I'll never know.

Kagran had its weak points—such as a strange venture to launch Howdy in Latin America. Efforts to produce a *Howdy Doody Show* with an all-Mexican cast fell apart when labor problems killed the deal. A Cuban *Howdy Doody Show* utilized a local cast teamed with duplicates of our puppets, sent from the United States. Instead of a Clarabell, they had a huge police dog, because they didn't believe Cuban children would appreciate a clown.

A Canadian *Howdy Doody Show*—local talent, duplicate puppets—enjoyed the distinction of enabling viewers in Detroit and Buffalo to watch two *Howdy* shows in a night, one from the United States, followed by another from across the border. It also gave Robert Goulet his first regular TV role—as Timber Tom, my Canadian counterpart.

Though Kagran had its weak points, it wasn't without its strong ones. It had, for instance, Eddie Kean in charge of new show development; and when Marty gave his brother, Allan Stone, a job with Kagran, I suggested that he hire my brother Vic.

Vic had sold his ski-ball business to a man in Newark, New York, when the fad essentially fizzled. From ski-

balls, he moved into Wurlitzer jukeboxes and phonographs. When he and his wife, Mary, visited Mil and me, they experienced TV for the first time. Vic worried, "Oh boy, these televisions will put my phonographs and jukeboxes out of business. Every bar in the world will have a TV." Back in Buffalo, he opened a TV emporium. But it was the worst time for inde-

. . . and as a Parisian painter in a smock.

pendents to try it. Consumers preferred to buy their sets from big department stores, in case this new fad blew over and they had to return their equipment. Besides, Vic would have had to buy a huge number of consoles in order to stock the few he could readily sell.

TV hardware let him down. TV software suited him better. He joined Kagran as Buffalo Vic. Marty signed up his father, Frank Stone, as Buffalo Frank. Together, Buffalo Vic and Buffalo Frank made outside appearances at amusement parks, sponsor functions, shopping center openings, and similar celebrations.

The creation of Buffalo Vic and Buffalo Frank stemmed from our success with road Clarabells. Poll Parrot, with two peak seasons for selling children's shoes—right before Easter and the last week in August—urged us to send Clarabell to their stores during those critical periods. We loved the idea, which promoted *The Howdy Doody Show* and the shoes simultaneously. We had as many as a dozen Clarabells on the road. When they appeared during the week, they made sure to leave in their Aerodoodles before our show aired, permitting the impression that the Clarabell on screen had just signed an autograph at your friendly downtown shoestore. One of these Clarabells died a while ago, in abject poverty. Papers, picking up the story, reported "Clarabell dead." To this day, the rumor that "the real Clarabell" passed away is almost as persistent as the one that Jerry "The Beaver" Mathers perished in Vietnam. (For proof that he didn't, consult tapes of our fortieth anniversary *Howdy Doody Show* in 1987. He sat in the Peanut Gallery with his offspring.)

One day Marty and Allan Stone and I went out to Queens to catch Buffalo Frank in a theater. Laurence Olivier had nothing to worry about. Frank tried, but we found his effort most embarrassing. After the show, Allan Stone glibly rose to his father's defense: "Well, I'll tell you, Bob. My dad may not be the greatest showman in the world, but he sure does a great job spot-cleaning a suit."

The Howdy whirl was great, though. Something doing every minute. Work, mostly. But lively, interesting work. I didn't mind not having much social life. None of us got out much. We worked grueling schedules and dragged ourselves home each night dead tired. Songwriters, hoping I'd play their tunes on my radio program and speed them toward Lucky Strike's *Hit Parade*, were lovely to me, showering me with tickets to some of the best musicals Broadway ever witnessed. *South Pacific. Annie Get Your Gun. Kismet.* I'd thank them, then give the tickets to friends, because I hadn't the energy to use them. One night I arrived home. Mil asked, "Did you give Broadway tickets

I didn't get to many Broadway shows, but I named my favorite dog after one of them. This is Happy Talk, my Welsh corgi, who was born during South Pacific.

away?" I admitted that I had. She warned, "Next time, ask me." After that I asked, went with her, and proceeded to sleep through *Brigadoon*, *My Fair Lady*, and I dread remembering what else.

Saturdays I'd spend with my sons, Ronnie and Robin, going to little league and practicing baseball. Sunday I spent at church, playing the organ, directing the choir, and serving as a devotional leader in Sunday school. A Sunday highlight would be visiting Eddie Joy, son of Georgie Joy, who headed the Santly-Joy music publishing company. The Joys had a terrific German cook named Paula. I spoke German with her, setting me high on her list of Joy guests. When we could go over—Mil, Ronnie, Robin, and I—we'd sit around the piano and sing. Sometimes Perry Como and his wife would be there, or Gordon and Sheila MacRae. We loved the food. We loved the socializing. We would have loved to do it more.

But when? Along with the *Howdy Doody* TV show, I had the radio program. At one point I had two radio programs, because we also had a *Howdy Doody* radio program. Twice I had two TV shows, once when I did *The Gulf Road Show* concurrent with *The Howdy Doody Show* and once when we took the best half hour from *The Bob Smith Show* on radio and shot it for daytime TV.

The *Howdy Doody* radio show was on the full NBC network, Satur-day mornings 9:00 to 10:00 A.M. Si Rady, former head of artists and repertoire at Decca Records, produced it. Si found Bob Cone to write it for us. It featured the Doodyville characters—Howdy, Dilly Dally, Mr. Bluster, the Flub-a-Dub, Judy Tyler as Princess Summerfall Winterspring, the whole gang—engaged in such tomfoolery as lousing up nursery rhymes. The princess might start, "Mary had a little lamb," and Dilly or the Flub-a-Dub or Mr. Bluster would cackle, "A lamb? What's she doing having a lamb? Only sheep have lambs."

We'd have musical sessions, among them numbers employing multiple dubs to form sixteen-piece orchestrations. By this I mean that Nick Nicholson and I would prerecord two instruments, then tape ourselves playing another two instruments along with the recording, and so on until we'd put sixteen instruments together—ranging from Nick's marvelous trombone to one or the other of us tooting kazoos, bike horns, whatever.

We also had Doc Whipple, our organist from the TV show; Frankie Carol, bass; Tony Mattola, guitar; Harry Brewer on the vibes and xylophones. Occasionally Harry tickled the keys of a buzzimba, a sort of marimba with a buzzing sound. Nick Nicholson wrote the backgrounds and arrangements. Each of these guys—a fine musician in his own right—contributed to the making of a great sound and a remarkable team.

Then we'd have a provocative question each week. After the *Howdy Doody* TV show was over, we'd bring the Peanuts and their parents across the hall to Studio 3A to tape their reactions to certain segments and interview them. One week I'd ask "If you could be any animal, what would you be?" Another week I'd want to know which famous parents they'd select if they could have a choice. We'd get thoughtful answers, clever answers, cute answers. Si would edit the best of them, and they'd go into our Howdy Doody radio show.

On one particular evening, I probed the kids, "Have you ever done anything wrong?" Then I followed up with, "And what did your mommy or daddy do to punish you?" I had thirty or forty children on stage, and a room full of parents, grandparents, aunts, and uncles in the audience. The kids wouldn't come across with anything juicy. I got "I took a pencil from brother." "Anything else?" "Nope." I realized that they wouldn't speak up for fear of betraying some secret their parents might not know about and getting spanked when they got home for something they did six months ago. So I said, "Look, kids, just make up something. Make up the worst thing in the world." I asked the audience, "You moms and dads don't mind, do you?" In one voice, they replied, "Naw."

I tried again: "What's your name, little fella?"

"Kenneth."

"Kenneth, did you ever do anything wrong?"

"I farted."

The audience went to pieces, burying their heads in their laps. The control room broke into giggle fits. Amazingly, I maintained my composure, until I got to the next lad:

"What's your name?"

"Teddy."

"Tedd-eee-hee-hee-hee-heeeeee . . ."

Nick Nicholson had to rescue me. He strolled over to me, stared down, and intoned in his Mr. Cobb voice, "Wha happin, Buffla Bob?" We had no option but to end the session and send everybody home.

That was the *Howdy Doody* radio show. The prime-time TV *Gulf Road Show*, initiated in September 1948, ran through three format changes in its first month and another two before we dropped it in June 1949. In succession, we had Enoch Light and his Light Brigade and also Johnny Guarnieri's orchestra. We did straight musical variety, a musical quiz format, a "What's New" series of inventions and talent, and audience participation. New talent included Patti Paige, Georgia Gibbs, Rosemary Clooney, and Jackie Gleason doing a comedy act and playing the trumpet.

Even with our pathetic budget for guests—a grand $50 per show—we managed nicely. Howdy visited occasionally, to catch up on gossip with me and to perform such numbers as "All

The Smiths love their music. That's Robin on the trumpet and Ronnie on the drums.

I Want for Christmas Is My Two Front Teeth." Billy Rose, a major guest by any standards, gladly appeared to plug his book. Kay Summersby, who had been General Eisenhower's secretary overseas during the war, brought rare film clips from the European theater of operation. She has since authored her own book—*Past Forgetting*—about her longtime love affair with the general.

Kay appeared in our studio mere minutes before our opening. She must have been either distracted or panicked, because when we asked her during narration, "And who is that man?" she said, "I have no idea." It was Eisenhower, big as life and clear as day.

The Gulf Road Show ended in 1949 and I quit my morning radio show in 1952, even though NBC built a radio studio in my basement to facilitate my continuing with it. But in 1954 word went out that Arthur Godfrey, in very poor health, would be giving up his morning radio show. NBC, sensing a good opportunity to enhance our radio ratings in the void that was certain to follow, put me on full network from 10:00 to 11:00 A.M. and on television from noon to 12:30. The TV offering was a condensation of the best half hour of the radio show.

We had a big band, directed by Nick Nicholson; we had the team of William Gilbert and Dr. Jack Weinstock (a brilliantly literate urologist), provided by MCA, to write for us; we had excellent musicians (including trombonists Ray Coniff and Will Bradley, trumpeter Red Solomon, guitarists Tony Gituso and Tony Mattola, and pianist Andy Ackers); a wonderful vocal group, the Honey Dreamers, composed of three men and two women; and we had a fine tenor in Clark Dennis. We did straight numbers, such as those in which Andy Ackers, Nick Nicholson, and I played three-piano arrangements; and comic spoofs. One, a take-off on renowned bandleader Fred Waring and his Pennsylvanians, we called Fried Herring and his Pencil Sharpeners. It came out half Fred Waring, half Spike Jones.

I'd kid Nick Nicholson that my band back in Buffalo was better than his, then brought out my little group of Smitty's Washboard Frolickers. The Frolickers played a washboard

and frying pans for a drum and cymbals; slide whistles and banjos; and a washtub jazzed up with a chord and two-by-four to sound like a bass fiddle. Nick Nicholson, Lew Anderson of the Honey Dreamers, and I would sing trio with the group, and our combo produced surprisingly melodious sounds.

Silly stuff. Homey stuff. Good stuff. I was proud of the show we did. Every morning we'd have a mystery memory year, and I'd begin with, for example, "Do you remember the year that the one dollar bill went from the large size to the small size? We thought we'd lose those small bills. But today we think those big bills look like bedsheets." I'd been doing this in Buffalo—long before Garry Moore did it on his prime-time program as "That Wonderful Year"—throwing out clues, holding up newspaper headlines, and performing tunes from the year. If it was the year the Charleston caught on, we might have the Honey Dreamers do it. Then I'd take the mike through the audience, and whoever guessed the year would win a prize.

I'd also interview the audience with a profound question of the day, such as "Who wears the pants in your family?" I'd speak to men and women, getting an assortment of funny answers, then wind up with Lew Anderson who we had planted in one of the seats. Dressed like a rube, he'd spring up and his name would always be Lou J. whatever we were asking about—in this example, "Lou J. Trousers," whereupon we'd launch into a comic exchange scripted by Gilbert and Weinstock.

Back in Doodyville, more changes. After Judy Tyler left, the Queen Great Grandmother of the Tinka Tonkas introduced several candidates for our new princess, ultimately played by Gina Gerardi. Gina did a fine job, was a fine person, had considerable talent.

In 1954 NBC completed the beautiful, modern, spacious Burbank Studios in Hollywood. Technically, New York City couldn't compare with what those studios offered. NBC originated several weekly prime-time shows from Burbank, but wanted to fully utilize their magnificent new equipment by

shooting a strip show—a daily show—out there as well.

They invited the entire *Howdy Doody Show* cast, along with writers, producers, production people, and everyone else, with a view toward our relocating permanently. Unfortunately, after four days, we couldn't wait to get back to New York. In TV terms, there was very little in California in 1954. The business still occurred in New York. If a client's commercial ran eight seconds over, there was nobody on the West Coast with enough authority to decide which eight seconds would be cut. We had to phone New York for everything, pacing the floor until calls were returned, and juggle the inconvenience of a three-hour time difference. On top of this, it rained incessantly.

Eddie Kean hadn't come out with us. He mailed us scripts from New York. Before we went back, we and Eddie arrived at the depressing conclusion that we needed to go our separate ways. After seven years, Eddie had exhausted the possibilities of Doodyville as far as he was concerned. What he wanted to write, we didn't want to perform. I don't blame him and he doesn't blame me, and our friendship remains intact. But lose Eddie we did, so we had to find new writers.

For a brief and unrewarding period, our part-time director Howard Davis wrote a handful of sad, sick, saccharine scripts focusing on, for in-

Happy, carefree childhood days as embodied by Princess Summerfall Winterspring, Clarabell (Nick Nicholson), and Sheriff Lanky Lou (Dayton Allen).

With Harpo Marx, shortly before Martin Stone confronted Groucho Marx.

stance, Howdy and his school teacher Miss Hickenlooper. I guess the name derived from Senator Hickenlooper, much in the news then. We were in a turmoil looking for writers. One of the writers who did several weeks of shows was Steve Krantz, husband of best-selling novelist Judith Krantz. In their wake came two gifted writers from the radio show, Willie Gilbert and Dr. Jack Weinstock. When Eddie wrote *The Howdy Doody Show*, he did the stories, the songs, and the music; but when Gilbert and Weinstock joined us, they confined themselves to scripts and lyrics, leaving the music to Nick Nicholson. Gilbert and Weinstock wrote differently than Eddie had—maybe hipper, where Eddie was cuter—but kids related to this team's

material as well. Years later, so did the Pulitzer Prize committee, when Gilbert and Weinstock collaborated with Abe Burrows to write the book for the 1961 Pulitzer Prize–winning Broadway musical *How to Succeed in Business Without Really Trying*.

The high point of our Burbank stay came when an array of big Hollywood names—including Red Skelton, Harpo Marx, and Jimmy Durante—agreed to share the stage with us for a March of Dimes special. Throughout the program, I ballyhooed the promised appearance of Groucho Marx. After getting the word that Groucho had arrived, I couldn't contain my enthusiasm: "Well, folks, he's here. He's just behind the curtain. Groucho Marx will be out any minute!" But Groucho, still hanging around the

THE BEAT GOES ON ————————————————

Mil and I laugh it up with Groucho Marx at the Burbank Studios following the March of Dimes Show, January 1954.

outside lobby, was in no hurry. Instead of rushing toward the cameras, he got into a conversation with Mil, who did her best to ease him toward the stage.

Marty Stone ran out to exert his own brand of pressure. Groucho, annoyed by the prodding, demanded, "Who are you?"

Marty asserted stolidly, "Who am I? I am *Martin Stone!*"

Groucho, obviously impressed, answered, "Well, fuck you, Martin Stone."

I finally managed the on-air interview by taking the show out to the lobby. Groucho allowed as how he hadn't really come to do the program. He'd only wanted to see Princess Summerfall Winterspring.

When we'd had as much fun as we could stand in Burbank, we made a beeline for New York.

Know what? All along I'd been conning myself that I thrived on pres-

---

HOWDY AND ME

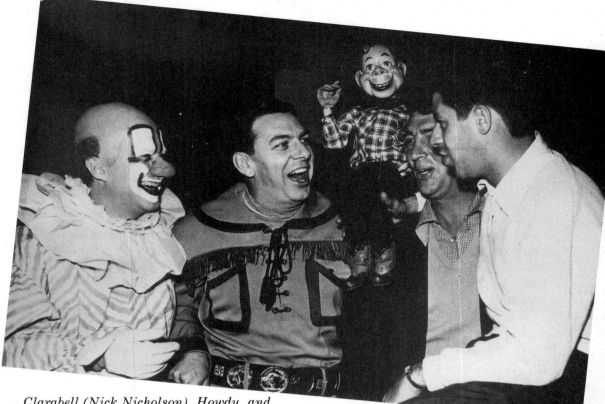

Clarabell (Nick Nicholson), Howdy, and I appear with Dean Martin and Jerry Lewis on their show, January 1954, at El Capitan Theatre, Hollywood, California.

sure up to the eyeballs, but perhaps I was wrong and it didn't entirely agree with me.

My schedule beginning in spring 1954 had me up at 6:00 A.M., driving by to pick up Clark Dennis at 7:00 since he lived on my way into the city, rehearsing like dervishes for the radio show then performing it 10:00 to 11:00, after which we immediately prepared for the daytime Bob Smith TV show. Then did the TV show. Then socko, got ready for *The Howdy Doody Show*. Then did *Howdy*. *Howdy*, as ever,

held strong, while our radio ratings climbed, climbed, climbed. We auditioned for General Mills and were about to be all sold out.

According to an August 8, 1954, NBC press release, "Summertime, and the living is easy—for some radio and TV personalities. With their programs off the air till fall, many take to the hills or to the seashore and with a minimum of phone calls, press interviews, scripts to memorize and rehearsals to attend they live a life of relative ease. Not so for Bob Smith. For seven summers he has worked straight through. . . . The thought alone of such frequent and far-ranging

THE BEAT GOES ON ——————————————————

activity is enough to make a strong man wilt, even in the cool of winter. But Bob grows strong on it, enjoying himself as much as his audience enjoys him every minute he is on the air."

A month after the press release, on the Sunday before Labor Day to be exact, I read through the week's scripts as usual. I would try every Sunday to mark and edit the whole week in advance, but rarely reached the goal. On this Sunday, I finished and delightedly announced to Mil, who was then seven and a half months pregnant with our son Christopher, "I'm done. It's the first time I've done that in ages." Mil and I had a few gin and tonics, ate outdoors, and went to bed at our regular hour, a madcap 9:00 P.M.

I woke up at 5:00 A.M., not in pain, but aware that I had no control. I went to the bathroom, lost every kind of control, made a mess, and surrendered to a crushing, excruciating agony that refused to abate. It felt like trucks backing up across my chest. Mil brought a shot of whiskey, forcing me to swallow. She phoned our internist who, even though it was Labor Day, called a cardiologist and appeared within seven minutes. The cardiologist arrived in another minute or two. Then came the ambulance.

The doctor gave me a shot of morphine, which alleviated the pain instantly. I said, "Gee, you've got to call Clark Dennis. Tell him I'll be a little late this morning." I was late—about four months late. I don't remember a single event from that point until I awoke in the hospital three days later.

Mil phoned NBC, explaining that I was in bad shape. It was at least seven o'clock before I was well enough to be put into the ambulance. When I came to my senses in the hospital, on oxygen and running a high fever, I felt lucky to be alive. Mil told me that NBC had assured her I had one job and only one job to do, which was to get better. They would pay me every week. In some professions, men got coronaries and couldn't earn their livelihoods at precisely the moment when they most urgently needed income. Naturally, this financial jeopardy added to their worries, making recovery something of a miracle. That September, if someone had promised me another thirty years in exchange for everything I owned or ever would own, it would have been a done deal. But NBC said, "Don't worry. Just get better." They didn't have to, and I'm grateful.

I did my best. I'd been in oxygen for two weeks before the fever subsided. My therapy began when they told me I should "dangle." To dangle was major progress. It consisted of sitting on the side of the bed with two nurses holding me while I dangled my feet. I didn't dangle for more than a minute when I felt like I'd been running a hundred miles.

Another week passed, and either my back or kidneys hurt horribly. I called the nurse, who called the doc-

A quieter moment at home in New Rochelle with Mil, Ron (left center), and Robin (right center). Milt Neil did the oil painting in the background.

tor, and I got a shot of Demerol. The needle barely entered my arm when I said, "I can't see." Boom. Again. I went out, thanks to anaphylactic shock, which I subsequently learned almost never occurs from Demerol. But I got it.

I revived four hours later, to see Mil's mother and Mil standing over me in her nightgown and mink coat. They'd phoned them to come right away, thinking I might not make it. After this, Mil came to see me every day, generally twice a day. In October

THE BEAT GOES ON —————

Our son Christopher.

Mil and I learned to relax. Here we are at the jai alai games in Dania, Florida.

our doctor said, "Ordinarily I'd let Bob go home now, but Mil could have her baby any day, and it would be sort of cute if you were in the hospital together. Cute and sensible. You can visit each other." Instead of going home mid-October, I waited in the hospital for Christopher to be born.

Christopher procrastinated. Finally Mil's doctor informed me, "I don't think she's going to have that baby as long as you're in the hospital. You're going home today."

I said, "Oh, great." It was, appropriately, Halloween. I felt like something they'd scooped out of a pumpkin to make a jack-o'-lantern. That's not quite fair, but I did feel incredibly weak. Mil and the nurse took me home in an ambulance and—what else?—Mil went into labor at four the next morning. She woke me to say she was leaving for the hospital in a cab. Her mother stayed behind to look after the three Smith men; the doctor

HOWDY AND ME

phoned at six with the news that there was another.

It was terrific. I couldn't have been more thrilled, and the heart attack did give me more time alone with my family. In those days, you simply didn't exert yourself after a heart attack. I never left the house. The doctor visited every two or three days, doing an EKG every week. One afternoon he stopped by as I took five phone calls in rapid succession. He got angry: "Who tended to those while you were in the hospital?" I guessed somebody else must have. He snapped, "Somebody else is going to take care of them now. You and Mil get out of here, go somewhere that this isn't going on."

We went to Florida, leaving six-week-old Chris, Robin, and Ronnie with our housekeeper, Gulli Inga Maj Jonason, and her husband, Alfonse, until the Christmas holidays. Both Maj and Al were wonderful with the kids, unstinting in their genuine affection and giving them the best of care.

I won't say I worried about money because I had more than my family needed, and certainly more than I had time to spend. On the other hand, the Kagran deal hadn't worked out too well. Whenever I asked Marty about Kagran's financial picture, he'd tell me everything was great, fabulous, and dandy. Then I'd ask if we were getting close to redeeming the debenture bonds, and we never were.

I'd gotten concerned enough in 1952 to consider licensing Buffalo Bob

on my own. I'd sold the other Doodyville characters outright, but not Buffalo Bob. I mentioned this to Marty. Because it would have stirred trouble among Kagran's licensees, Kagran settled with me. Not for the character. Not for the copyright. They paid me an annual figure not to license Buffalo Bob. To my mind, this at least generated ready cash that I wasn't seeing from the Kagran operation.

By 1954 Kagran still hadn't redeemed the bonds. Then, in Florida in December, I got a call from NBC's Gus Margraf. NBC was buying out Marty's common stock in order to open their own licensing company, California National Productions, to license all NBC properties. I asked how much they bought Marty out for. Gus told me to guess. I surmised, "Well, I have $250,000 in debenture bonds coming. I'm going to guess $250,000." Gus replied, "You hit it right on the nose." (I wasn't surprised—though enor-

This is part of Pioneer Village in my New Rochelle basement.

mously delighted—when NBC and California National turned the licensing around and redeemed my bonds within the next year.)

We left Florida at the end of the winter holiday, to get Robin and Ronnie back to school. By the time we returned home, Howdy's sponsors made it known that they were nervous. They wanted me back. After the heart attack, my radio show had gone on only another three months without me. The *Bob Smith* TV program, which was hosted by Ernie Kovacs, Skitch Henderson, and several others, also folded. Howdy kept on uninterrupted, but let's face it, I belonged with Howdy.

In my absence Allen Swift had done Howdy's voice. At first, they tried my brother Vic, whose voice is indistinguishable from mine. When Vic was in the service and I phoned home—"Hello, Ma"—my mother would brighten up and give me an animated "Hello, Victor, honey, how are you?" Then I'd correct her, and get a flat "Oh, Robert, how are you?" I used to tease her about that. So NBC tried Vic. Evidently he could have done a good me, but he couldn't pick up on Howdy's inflections. Puppeteer Allen Swift practiced, came the closest, and got the job. But because he couldn't sing, Howdy gave up singing for the duration. Howard Davis or his son contends that, according to some, Allen did Howdy's voice better than I

did. Is that like saying Perry Como does the Bing Crosby voice better than Bing Crosby? I'm stymied. In any event, the sponsors wanted me back doing Howdy's voice.

I confronted my doctor, who allowed me to return to *The Howdy Doody Show* on condition that I do it from my own home and not battle the rat race into and out of New York City.

A studio already existed in my basement, left over from my early-morning radio show. We got a camera down there, a seven-foot grand piano, a Hammond organ, and converted the radio studio into one for television. In terms of a story line, we needed a reason for me to be in a setting other than the usual studio. Insoluble? Not to Eddie Kean who, from his post with Kagran, suggested that we decorate my basement as a Pioneer Village. All along, the parents of America knew about my heart attack. They saw the newspapers. But as far as the kids had been told, Buffalo Bob was away on a secret mission. During my absence, guest hosts and the Doodyville gang read letters from me on the air. In the interim, Gabby Hayes subbed for me, as did Jimmy Blaine, Rex Marshall, and Ted Brown. Ted Brown—still on WNEW today—introduced himself as Bison Bill. Tim McCutcheon showed up as Timothy Tremble.

In a major behind-the-scenes transformation, Nick Nicholson hung up his zebra-striped Clarabell suit for

And me trying *to relax.*

the last time. Nick had been appealing to us right along. "Guys, this was supposed to be temporary. I don't want to wear that costume and makeup all day. I don't want to make personal appearances on weekends. I am definitely not comfortable. You really ought to let me off the hook." He and I and Roger talked it over and had to agree. He wore as many hats as Corny Cobb and did more than his fair share. Needing another Clarabell, we lassoed Lew Anderson.

Roger asked Lew, "Would you like to be Clarabell?"

The ever-honest Lew said, "I don't know. I never saw it."

"Wanna try the costume?"

"Okay."

Lew Anderson stepped into the outfit and makeup. When Nick Nicholson saw Lew, he proclaimed him an instant clown. Lew recalls, "Once I had the costume and makeup on, the stage hands couldn't tell the difference."

Roger said, "We'll write you in for two days, and you'll start."

Lew inquired, "Start what?"

"Can you juggle?"

"No."

"Do magic tricks?"

"No."

"What can you do?"

"Nothing."

"That's perfect. If you make mistakes, that's in character. Clarabell always makes mistakes."

Lew considered studying old kinescopes, but Roger instructed him to go his own route. The advice paid off. Lew enthralled us, inspired only by his duds and residence in Doodyville. He explains, "Once you get into the costume, you do things you wouldn't otherwise do." But it is inaccurate to suggest that he did "nothing" as Clarabell. We were able to take full advantage of his musicianship, and couldn't have been more proud to reveal that Clarabell played the clarinet and, like Nick, was a great musician and arranger.

Before, during, and after portraying TV's Clarabell, Lew continued to perform as a musician, as well as to write some of the most popular commercial product jingles of the Fifties. (Remember "Pepsi Cola hits the spot" and "Wouldn't you really rather have a Buick?" They were his, and the vocal

group in the commercials was his group, the Honey Dreamers.) On personal appearances, he continues as Clarabell with me to this day. His only complaint seems to be "When I'm not in clown makeup and my zebra-striped suit and people hear I'm Clarabell, it infuriates me that they respond, 'Oh, sure, now I recognize you.'"

On camera, 1954 had been a busy year in Doodyville, with our re-re-placing Clarabell, searching for a new princess, hunting for a platinum platypus, rescuing Captain Windy Scuttlebutt from the clutches of a magician who rendered him invisible, dashing off to Mother Goose Land, rounding up new animals for the circus (Tommy the Turtle voiced by Lew Anderson, Paddle the Gnu, Mambo the Elephant, Hyde and Zeke, Tiz the Dinosaur, and Buzz Beaver), and contending with Sandy MacTavish when he tried to build a kippered herring plant in Doodyville Park. At this juncture, Buffalo Bob traveled to Paris to find a history book that would decide ownership: Did the park belong to Doodyville or to Chief Thunderthud? I disappeared in Paris and turned up in—

Pioneer Village! Inasmuch as I had to have the heart attack anyhow, this proved to be a handy point in the story to have it. I pursued my secret mission, while Doodyville unraveled the ownership mystery. It seems my ancestors had given a portion of the land to Chief Thunderthud, who had the right to relinquish that turf to

MacTavish. But the chief's teepee and Bluster's house stood there already, leaving MacTavish no other option than to skedaddle.

I returned to *The Howdy Doody Show*, via remote control from Pioneer Village, in January 1955. Bison Bill and Mr. Nick (Nick Nicholson) co-hosted with me, until Bison Bill departed to serve as superintendent of Clown Town, a position formerly filled by Mr. Nick. One day Clarabell would come to my house, another day Oil Well Willie, another day Zippy. Throughout, the camera caught glimpses of me on my secret mission. "Now, look, kids, I'm on a great mission here in Pioneer Village. And I start the day right. I have Kellogg's Rice Krispies for breakfast, and brush with Colgate Dental Cream"—or words to that effect.

My mission continued until Labor Day 1955, at which time we went from black-and-white to color. The color process had unique significance at NBC, the TV and radio subsidiary of RCA—the most successful early manufacturer of color television sets. NBC's chairman, General David Sarnoff, ushered in the new era with the flattering observation that inasmuch as Milton Berle and Howdy Doody were responsible for selling so many millions of televisions when TV began, Howdy's program had earned the honor to be the first on the air each day to promote color TV. Moreover,

---

J. Cornelius Cobb (Nick Nicholson), Captain Windy, Flub-a-Dub, Dr. Singasong (Bill LeCornec).

inasmuch as NBC's test patterns would have to incorporate color, Howdy's face would appear in them. This way, if a TV serviceman arrived at your door to install a color set at 9:30 A.M., he'd have something to tune the set to, in order to be sure it functioned properly.

NBC knocked down the walls between two studios at 30 Rock—studios 3G and 3H—renaming them 3K, with the *K* standing for Kolor. The quality of our color really impressed me. In those days, if you watched a ballgame, you might get yellow grass, red grass, blue grass. Very hairy. That happened because lighting changed and couldn't be controlled, and because cameras had to follow the ballplayers' actions instantly, with no time to adjust equipment other than to reposition it. But on Howdy's set, we had controlled conditions and the same technicians each day. We therefore had extraordinarily rich, lifelike hues. Unfortunately, we couldn't save any tapes of our show. Tape cost too much. Instead of shelving the footage, everyone reused it, recording one show over the next.

Color entailed certain costume modifications. My original Buffalo suit had been beige trimmed in brown. Then we went to a light-blue outfit trimmed in dark blue. Beautiful. Gorgeous. But when we went to color, we employed Chroma-key. Chroma-key is the special effects process that enables an actor to stand in front of a blue background waving his arms, while another background is electronically substituted behind him. The finished product has the actor flying over the Grand Canyon or through outer space, because the camera had been programmed not to "see" blue and therefore to eliminate the first background. In my case, my body became the background. With Chroma-key, my head bobbed along without benefit of neck or torso. So we got as far away from blue as we could, and I started wearing a yellowish-orange costume trimmed in red, with gray fringe.

For color, Arlene Dalton replaced Gina, not as a Tinka Tonka princess but as our Story Princess. Arlene's gorgeous gowns had breathtaking impact in color, though her stories and poems may have been too tame for our audience. The kids had come to expect slapstick and Clarabell's spritzing people, which these quiet tales failed to deliver.

The color adventures of Doodyville proper began with a little girl puppet saving me from drinking poisoned water in Africa. When I brought her back to Doodyville, mean Mr. Bluster cited a law that nobody could move into town unless related to a resident. Accordingly, Howdy arranged to have Heidi become his adopted sister, Heidi Doody (voiced by our own Story Princess, Arlene Dalton). Shortly after, Dilly Dally and Heidi required rescuing from the planet Neptune, and our audience discovered

Still trying . . .

the flying Bloop, who appeared when anyone spoke a word with an *oop* rhyme in it.

Beyond the saga, we switched from old-time movies to color cartoons, ran travel films by Lowell Thomas, Jr., and welcomed Corny Cobb back to reopen his general store.

My personal saga shifted into higher gear. Needing technology more advanced than anything available in Pioneer Village, I had to return to New York City. I flashed back to endless memories of rush hour and

backed-up traffic. One particularly came to mind, of a night when Mil phoned to tell me that roads would be unbelievably bad from the snow on the ground, "So don't hurry. Take your time. We won't worry about you. Don't you worry about us. Just be careful, and we'll have a fire going when you get back."

It was always bumper to bumper on Friday afternoons at least as far north as the George Washington Bridge in upper Manhattan, where it tended to thin out. But this Friday, nothing moved. It couldn't have been

THE BEAT GOES ON —————————————

slower, or worse. Traffic was horrible in both directions. By seven thirty I'd just about made it to the bridge. Because studio lights were so hot in those days, we used to drink quite a lot of water and orange juice. Now the beverages made their demands on me, in a traffic jam three lanes wide each way. What to do? I had my trombone in the trunk of the car. My car was stopped anyway, so I went out, opened the trunk, opened my trombone case, and removed the mute. I brought the mute back to the front seat with me and used it. When I rolled the window down and emptied the mute, everyone knew what I'd done. It was a dark winter night, therefore all sorts of lights were on. Drivers, at a standstill, with nothing to do, couldn't help noticing me. Almost in unison they began to honk their horns. I think they wanted to borrow the mute. Personally, I'm grateful I didn't play the piccolo.

Consequently, when the boss said I'd better leave Pioneer Village and start commuting to the city again, I wasn't happy. Fortunately, he added, "Bob, be easy on yourself. Don't fight traffic every day. Buy a limousine, and get somebody to drive you."

I didn't have to think twice about who my driver would be. Years before Dayton Allen and I had been heading home on the West Side Highway. We drove together because he lived in Mt. Vernon, not far from my place. We must have been exceeding the speed limit by a few miles, because a motorcycle policeman, Karl Petersen, pulled us over on a little traffic island. He stopped us and one other car. While he spoke to the other driver, I took my registration from the glove compartment, put it in my pocket, flustered, and forgot that I'd grabbed it. When Officer Petersen asked me for my registration and operator's license, I could produce the license from my wallet, but drew a blank on the registration.

He proceeded to question me. Who was I? Where did I work? I told him I was in radio and television. He wanted to know "Doing what?" I said I was on *The Howdy Doody Show*, and he said, "Ohmigosh! You're Buffalo Bob!" I confessed, then introduced him to Dayton. "This is Dayton Allen, who is Ugly Sam, Pierre the Chef, Lanky Lou, and the voices of Mr. Bluster and the Flub-a-Dub." Dayton obliged by doing recitations of all his characters.

I added, "Officer, as a personal reference, I have a card from Mr. James Burke, Borough President of Queens, with whom I made a benenfit appearance a month ago."

Officer Petersen replied, "Well I don't think my son would like it if I gave Buffalo Bob a citation, but you were speeding. I must give you a warning. In fact, several. First, get your registration in order. If it's lost, you'd better report it. Second, you've got to stick to the speed limit. And

No, this isn't Pete and me commuting to New York in traffic. It's Buffalo Bob Day in Buffalo, New York 1952.

third, you've got to get another friend in politics. Jim Burke isn't going to run again next year."

Karl "Pete" Petersen and I shook hands and subsequently became good friends. We'd wave to each other on the highway, or if he had a fellow officer with him, he'd stop me to say hi. He came to my house. Dayton and I went to parties to entertain when Pete's pals became sergeants—they called these celebrations "rackets." Pete's son visited *The Howdy Doody Show.*

Pete was without a doubt one of the most intelligent men I ever knew,

and a credit to the force. I therefore felt particularly miserable to hear that he'd had a motorcycle accident in spring 1955 when his wheels hit a patch of gravel spread over a layer of ice. The NYPD awarded Pete a permanent disability, retiring him.

So at the words "Get a limo, get a driver," I phoned Pete, offering him the job. Then I contacted my golf buddy J. Paul Carey of Carey Limousine, who delivered a black Cadillac limo at fleet price. Pete found a beautiful bar at Abercrombie & Fitch, built a stand for it, and installed gimbal rings to hold the glasses. On the way home from work in the evening, we'd have Ovaltine on the rocks.

THE BEAT GOES ON —————————

Okay, I admit that I worked in the limo. Roger Muir lived in Pelham, Nick Nicholson in Larchmont, and I in New Rochelle. Every night we'd come home together after *The Howdy Doody Show*. Naturally, we covered all sorts of business along the way. But in style. We even had air conditioning.

Thanks to the air conditioning, I could relax in the backseat with the windows up and a cool breeze blowing on the hottest of days. One weekend afternoon, Mil and I sat in the backseat with drinks in our hands, while Robin and Ronnie sat up front with Pete so

that their Little League uniforms wouldn't soil the rear upholstery. A wreck of a car crawled up beside us. The driver, sweating bullets, a kerchief tied around his neck, signaled us to roll down the window. When we did, he observed, "Must be a whole lot of money in that baseball. . . ."

On another occasion—a scorchingly hot night—Pete and I came up behind my attorney, Pat O'Hara, on the East River Drive. Cars idled bumper to bumper. People looked like they lacked the strength to get home.

I stirred up a stiff gin and tonic, popped a lime in it, and had Pete pull up parallel to Pat. When Pat stopped again, so did we.

I stuck my head through the window to ask, "How much would you give for a gin and tonic?"

Pat gasped, "A hundred bucks."

Handing him the drink, I said, "Send me a check in the morning."

Horns all around us began honking. Drivers shouted out orders. "I'll have a highball!" "Two Manhattans here!" I had to duck back inside. They mistook us for a traveling bar.

When I got home and told Mil, we decided it deserved a song. We wrote:

We bought a car.
In the back there's a bar.
Now we're driving ourselves to
*   drink.*

THE BEAT GOES ON —————————————————————

6

THE MOUSE TRAP

*N*ow *The Howdy Doody Show* was loaded with talent, and could really do some intelligent production numbers along with our cartoons and our Doodyville derring-do. The show had a new look, particularly when I came back Labor Day of 1955.

By then we'd produced nearly two thousand *Howdy Doody Show* telecasts and for years were rated the most popular five-times-a-week daytime show on television. We'd received the Peabody Award; educators lavished praise on our commitment to "constructiveness and educational aspects"; and the Spanish-language family magazine *Temas* described Doodyville as "the only paradise never lost: the children's paradise. Howdy has become as famous as Pinocchio or as any of the fiction characters who inhabit the golden world of children." Our viewing audience exceeded 5 million.

Not surprisingly, no children's programming ever attempted to pry into Howdy's rating. Everything went our way, virtually unchallenged, for a long time. A long time. But not forever. It took Walt Disney to come up with the great *Mickey Mouse Club*, which ran a full hour, 5:00 to 6:00 P.M., on ABC. Back then we considered ABC an upstart network. It's not that we didn't take it seriously, but we definitely didn't conceive of any "Big Three" networks. It was more like two and a half. Yet, with *The Howdy*

My path continues to cross with Mickey Mouse's. (Left to right, back) Alan Young, yours truly, Dave Nelson, Art Linkletter, Werner Klemperer, (front) Rose Marie, Annette Funicello, Imogene Coca, Morey Amsterdam, and Edie Adams are putting our handprints in cement for Disney/ MGM Studios Theme Park's salute to 50 years of television broadcasting.

Doody Show running on NBC from 5:30 to 6:00, Mickey got the jump on us. Look at the pool of talent they had. Wonderful numbers. Stunningly gifted kids. Disney cartoons. Kids who tuned into it at 5:00 could hardly be expected to tear themselves away for another program. And the *Mickey Mouse Club* was prefilmed, affording tremendous versatility, whereas Howdy played live. We may have had pretaped voices, or an occasional bit for the Super Talk-O-Scope, but our show itself was a live show. In short, Mickey put a dent in Howdy's supremacy.

THE MOUSE TRAP ——————

I'll never forget the day it hit me. Mil and I were in Clearwater, Florida. Glancing at an issue of *Variety*, I read that Howdy, "caught in a mouse trap," would be moved to Saturday mornings. The irony is that our ratings had never flagged. But major advertisers

DONNA: Early TV studios were a pain to work in. When did they get comfortable?

BOB: It was hot, dry, and dusty in those early days. We all had dust headaches by four o'clock. We'd raid the infirmary for Chlor-Trimeton and eat it like jellybeans. Just when the black-and-white cameras improved so we could work with cool lights, we went to color. The first color cameras needed more light than those early black-and-white jobs. It got hot all over again. The color studios didn't cool off until after Howdy left the air. Just couldn't win.

seeking fresh, new faces found them in Mickey, Donald, Goofy, and the Mouseketeers.

Mickey wasn't the only factor. Another was definitely that the late-afternoon time slot had taken on a new meaning in the eyes of sponsors. What had once been perceived as a kiddie hour—"Who's watching then except kids two to twelve years old?"—emerged as a period capable of drawing a much larger group. Kids. Teenagers. College students. Mothers. Singles. Grandparents. Why sell toothpaste to a small percentage of the population when you can sell cars to viewers aged twenty to ninety on a game show or afternoon talk show? Very simply, the whole picture changed.

The Howdy Doody Show, along with many other kids' shows, moved to Saturday morning. We got a prime spot, 10:00 to 10:30 A.M., and maintained strong ratings. We introduced Gumby. We added Kokomo Junior, another chimp; Sandra Witch, a puppet; Hazel Witch, a live one played by Nick Nicholson; and Peppy Mint, portrayed by Marti Barris. Marti's father, Harry, had been one of the Rhythm Boys with Bing Crosby. Marti, like Gina and Arlene, performed extremely well. I hate to say, but have to say, that as good as they were, we kept hoping we'd find another Judy Tyler.

Gilbert and Weinstock wrote for us at the time. They created Pesky the

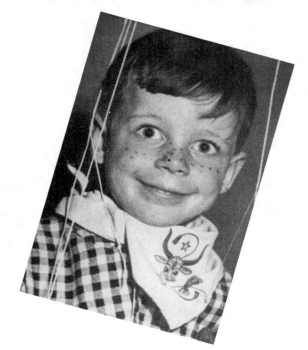

Billy Oltman, winner of the Howdy Doody look-alike contest.

Clown, played by Nick Nicholson, to be Clarabell's rival. Nick remembers the role well: "The kids hated Pesky. Really hated him. They wouldn't let anyone unseat Clarabell in their affections, so I hammed it up to the hilt, being this kind of Mr. Bluster of clowndom, and had a ball."

Howdy celebrated his tenth anniversary with a gala one-hour party on December 28, 1957, just as we reached our 2200th performance. All Howdy's friends joined us. Among our special guests were three kids who had been in the very first pre–Peanut Gallery, on December 27, 1947. NBC had spent quite a nice piece of change to find them—a teenage girl and boy who were twins, and another teenage girl.

We also had on that show the ten semi-finalists of our Howdy Doody "Most Winning Smile in America" contest, selected from hundreds of thousands of entries we'd received. I interviewed them all on the program, and I have to say that each one couldn't have been more adorable. The winner, Tammy Merrithew, later went on to do the *Robert Cummings Show*, and I've heard she's active in Hollywood to this day.

We'd had to let some members of the staff go when we went from five days a week to one, but even at that, we learned that TV's budgets had sky-rocketed in a matter of a few years. It was prohibitively costly to put on programs as expensive as *The Howdy Doody Show*. Not just the gala. Each and every one of them. To stage a show like ours, and pit it against Saturday morning cartoons, made for a losing proposition. It marked the end of an era.

Shari Lewis replaced us. I'm happy to say Roger Muir produced her show. It couldn't have cost a tenth of what Howdy cost. Shari, with her winning personality, worked alone with her hand puppets on a single set.

From a financial standpoint, I didn't have to worry. In one of my early contracts, Marty Stone negotiated that Howdy Doody would always be on the air between 4:30 and 6:00 P.M. When NBC rescheduled Howdy to Saturday morning, they apparently overlooked this stipulation. As a re-sult, the William Morris Agency was able to negotiate a new contract for me, specifying that I continue to receive the same $1,500 a week for one half-hour Saturday show that I'd gotten for five half-hour weekday shows, and *would* receive it until 1960, even if our program disappeared altogether. We also used the opportunity to reiterate contractually that I still owned the character of Buffalo Bob, the buckskin fringe, the voice, the personality. To people outside of the industry, it may sound silly to say that I retained the right to act as me. But of course, it implies a whole constellation of commercial possibilities—ranging from phonograph records to my making public appearances in costume.

So I got to be me, but that was it for Howdy. He outlasted *The Mickey Mouse Club*, which left the air in 1959. Now came Howdy's turn. This was no easy adjustment for any of us, but I have nothing to regret. With 2,543 programs under our combined belts, Howdy and I did our last show, a one-hour special, in September of 1960. When we started the hour, Clarabell held up a card that read *Surprise*. We spent the entire show trying to guess what he had in mind. We couldn't figure it out. He kept pestering us, then putting us off. We'd do something else, then try to get around Clarabell: "Come on, you should tell us. What's the surprise?" But he'd stall.

Finally, when we had about ten

seconds to go, he pantomimed to me that he could talk. Clarabell can talk? Well, Clarabell, do it. Hurry. Hurry up.

The camera dollied right into his face, a tight close-up. Lew Anderson's lips trembled as he sighed, "Good-bye, kids."

Not a dry eye could be seen in the studio.

Emotional as it was, we got over it quickly, because we'd taped the last couple of years' shows, and we'd taped this one about three weeks in advance. After we shot it, we had a big party, convinced that our contracts would be renewed and we'd be back.

We thought surely Howdy would return in six months or a year, and that we were just taking a vacation. I'd had the firm pay-or-play contract with NBC through 1960. If I had to guess, I would have figured the sudden cessation of Doodyville to be a bargaining ploy. I never doubted for a minute that we'd be around as long as Pinocchio and Little Orphan Annie.

For me, the sad part came three weeks later, when the show aired on September 23. Mil and Chris and I sat in our sun room. When Clarabell said, "Good-bye, kids," I looked at six-year-old Chris. Tears streamed down his cheeks. I glanced over at Mil.

Same reaction. Was it possible that there would be no reprieve? It was Saturday morning, and I beat it out of the house, drove to Bonnie Briar Country Club, and played the worst round of golf of my life.

And then nothing. No renewals. Not even a gold Howdy Doody watch.

I repeat, I have no regrets. But it dawned on me at the fairly tender age of forty-three that, for the first time ever, I had seemingly infinite leisure. To all intents and purposes, my only contact with Doodyville days after 1960 was likely to be an occasional appearance as Buffalo Bob on Johnny Carson's show, Merv Griffin's, or Mike Douglas's.

Rather than goof off, I paid more attention to other ventures I'd gotten into, such as the liquor store I bought when Howdy went from five shows to one. I'd done that largely because, when I had to let staff go, I didn't want to lose my association with Pete Petersen. Along with driving my car, after a while he'd served as a production assistant for us. With our Howdy connection dissolving, Pete and I decided to go into another business together. So we graduated from the bar in the limo to a full-fledged liquor

🐭 *Here Howdy and I celebrated Christmas 1953. Almost four years to the day later, we celebrated our 2200th performance. Not many months beyond that, we left the air.*

store. I don't think the previous owner had done too well with it, and I acquired it for a figure equivalent to a year of the man's gross. I opened it across the street from my brother Vic's shoe store—a business Vic got into after appearing as Buffalo Vic in so many Poll Parrott operations that he developed an affinity for shoes. What hooked him, I think, were slipperdoodles—slippers with Doodyville characters on the instep. Kids would squeeze them and the toys would make little noises.

In New Rochelle, people would say, "See the Smith Brothers for shoes and booze." Or "boots and booze."

Pete ran the liquor store for me with Vito Racine, Ray Doran, and Osburne Young. We were all born young, but his name was Osburne. They must have done something right, because we increased our volume tremendously.

On the subject of neighborhoods, a young boy, Burt Dubrow, resided in ours, though at the other side of town. Describing him as a Howdy Doody fan doesn't do him justice. Howdy Doody absolutely hypnotized him. When Burt learned that Buffalo Bob had a boozery in New Rochelle, he would take the bus to our liquor store to chat with me. Frequently. Then incessantly. He'd come to the store, asking for tickets and autographs. He'd bring his friends, introducing them and assuring them of autographs. Vic hired him to wait on customers in the shoe store. He and Vic got along famously. After

THE MOUSE TRAP

a while I'd hide in the back of my store when I saw Burt coming down the street. I liked him tremendously, so it must be that I felt trapped. If this was being trapped, I recommend it highly—but more on this later.

During those years Mil and I got into the habit of spending our summers in Maine, which I discovered virtually by accident to be our own private version of Nirvana. In the late Forties, I had my hair cut in the subbasement of the NBC building at 30 Rockefeller Plaza. The State of Maine Publicity Bureau had its office next door to the barbershop. In 1950 NBC sent me for a month's vacation. Feeling decidedly under the weather, I welcomed the break. After a haircut one day, I walked into the State of Maine bureau. I liked to fish, and Mil did—ever since the afternoon after church on my uncle's farm when she hooked and landed a four-pound rainbow trout—and I'd heard about really fine fishing in Maine.

I must say the State of Maine did right by us. I said, "We have a month coming to us. I want to start it off with a week of solitude, quietude, no cocktail partytude. Where do we go to fish?"

The ladies answered, "Washington County, Maine."

I asked them to book a reservation. They called five or six places, each of which was booked solid. Then they contacted Grand Lake Stream Lodge, run by an old vaudevillian

With Ted Williams and 17 pounds of smallmouth bass caught with fishing rods from his new line of equipment, which he'd just sold to Sears. Great Lake Stream, Maine.

named Artie MacKenzie. When Art heard that Mil and I needed lodgings, he promised us the guest room in his home until he could get us a cabin.

·We loved it. Love at first sight. We went out in a canoe with our guide, Hazen Bagley, probably boring him with our tales of scripts and responsibilities and how relieved we were to have left them behind. As much as I cherished the privilege of being Buffalo Bob and performing with Howdy and the Doodyville gang, it was good to be somewhere that none of it meant a thing to a blessed soul. TVs in that part of Maine in 1950 simply did not receive *The Howdy Doody Show.*

HOWDY AND ME

Yet when we put to shore at four-thirty, fifty kids awaited us at the dock. They'd heard Buffalo Bob was in town. They knew about Howdy through the comic books and through visiting their relatives, and vacationers up from New York and Boston had seen the shows from the beginning.

Mil and I liked Maine so much that we canceled our other plans and stayed with Artie and Hazen for the rest of the month. We haven't missed a year in Maine since 1950. In the autumn of 1957, we built our own home there. It's very refreshing, very different from New York and Florida, very New England. By this I mean that the people don't say any more than they have to say. They're taciturn from birth. Where other babies are encouraged when they start speaking, I half suspect that Maine babies are cautioned, "Don't get carried away."

The first time we made the trip, Mil and I left New Rochelle at 8:00 in the morning. There were no thruways then, so it took us until 11:00 P.M., and passing through every bitty town on the map. Unsure about the condition of the road between Lincoln and Topsfield, I stopped at a gas station and asked an attendant, "How is that road?"

He said, "Crooked," and went back inside.

One of the local residents is a full-blooded Passamaquoddy Indian whose Christian name is Mary Teresa, but everyone knows her as Buffalo Mary. I introduced myself to her in the store after I'd lived in town for several years, though we'd never actually met or spoken. I said, "You know, you and I have the same name."

She asked matter of factly, "Your name Teresa?" She pronounced it Treesa; a golfing buddy of mine, Dr. Chuck Bonura, has referred to me as Treesa ever since.

A friend of ours, Bill White, sold bait. Consequently, a visit to Bill headed the list of things to do upon each year's return to Maine. One year when we left, Bill's wife had been seriously ill. When I saw him the following May, I inquired after her health.

Bill replied, "Wife passed away in December."

Fishing again, this time with Bert Lahr (the Cowardly Lion of Wizard of Oz *fame). We're in front of my home in Maine.*

I extended my condolences, profoundly sorry to learn that she hadn't pulled through.

Bill continued sadly, "Yup. Now it's just my dog and me." Pause. "No, wait a minute. Dog died in March. Now it's just me."

Because I'm a member of the Rotary Club, I attend meetings regularly. Those are their rules. If you're not in your hometown, you ring up the local chapter and go there. It's an excellent system—a perfect way to come in contact with people from a variety of professions all around the world. One week, finding myself in Calais, Maine, I went to their meeting, sat next to a Dr. Hazen Mitchell, and instantly hit it off with him. Mitch was an impressive guy, one of two doctors in Calais. He and Dr. Sears would do a tonsillectomy in the morning, set a leg in the afternoon, and deliver babies before dinner. They were the town surgeons, family doctors, the works.

Mitch and I became golfing buddies, while his wife, Katrine, became a bridge chum of Mil's. One day in 1964 Mitch phoned bursting with excitement, telling me that the local radio station was for sale. WQDY—its call letters derived from the Passamaquoddy Indians of the region—was available because the man who owned it had to raise cash, in order to start a cable TV operation. Mitch said, "You love radio. It's right up your alley."

I looked into it, discussing details with the owner, John von Dell, with his sales manager, Dan Hollingdale, and his accountant, Joseph Bothwick. The station grossed $75,000 a year. John von Dell asked $100,000 for it, a bargain. The usual going rate for a station in that part of the country would be two or three times the year's gross. Von Dell took me to his home, which also happened to contain the station. He had the station, the studio, the equipment, everything, in his home on Main Street. When I agreed to $100,000, he said, "Fine. However, the house will be extra. And I want you to notice that I put in new rugs."

"How much extra?"

"Ten thousand dollars." No problem. Today the house alone is worth a hundred thousand.

Mil and I needed $125,000 in cash—$110,000 for von Dell and $15,000 for working capital. We formed a corporation and had the corporation borrow $100,000, which we personally secured. We modernized. Eventually we went AM/FM. We retired all our indebtedness in four or five years and increased our gross to over $500,000 a year. It turned out to be one of the best investments I ever made. Besides, think of the fun.

Another of my favorite sports, with some of my favorite sports greats: Mickey Mantle, Yankee general manager Roy Hamey, and Yogi Berra. Florida 1957.

It was real local radio. We'd have talent shows and area celebrities. We'd have special programs, such as a Radio Rotary Day, on a July Saturday when most people were home. We'd donate the advertising time to the local Rotary, which would sell the spots to butchers, bakers, candlestick makers—whoever—much the way that neighborhood concerns sponsor ads in high school yearbooks.

Naturally, we didn't do this straight. We got commercial. We'd have the president of the electric company doing an ad for oil, and the president of the gas company lauding the virtues of electric power. We'd have the head of one bank praising his rivals. And we had doctors Mitchell and Sears, both very good singers, waxing melodic about one another. To the tune of "Bye, Bye, Blackbird," Dr. Sears crooned:

Measles, mumps, or chicken pox,
Who's the greatest of the docs?
Doctor Mitchell . . .

Hazen Mitchell returned the favor with:

Who is it that babies all cry for?

CHORUS: *Dr. Sears.*

Who is it that all the germs die for?

CHORUS: *Dr. Sears.*

Mil and I wrote the parodies. Then we'd ask for pledges, because Dr. Mitchell had brought his saxophone. When Dr. Mitchell played the saxophone, it sounded awful, like something full of bees. We asked for pledges to amount to $100 for Mitch to play the sax. Then people would phone in pledges for $200 for Mitch *not* to play the sax. They had the same reaction when he offered to play a Hammond Organ instead.

Not only did we wind up with residents happy and interested in the station, but we conveyed the message that this was their best means of communication. If school let out early, if there was a danger of tainted food in a grocery store, if volunteers were needed at an accident site in a hurry, newspapers failed completely. But radio spread the message within minutes. One good friend of ours, Smitty Thomas, had an aneurism. It burst. The doctors worked on him feverishly for fourteen hours. The Calais hospital, short on his blood type, contacted Bangor. Bangor had it, but couldn't get it to him in time. We broadcast the story on our radio station. Fifty volunteers appeared within five minutes, providing more than enough blood to save his life. Today Smitty is well and healthy—thanks to radio, some devoted, talented, and dedicated doctors, and good neighbors.

It goes without saying that this feature of local radio is one of the most gratifying, and why I feel so strongly about it.

THE MOUSE TRAP ——————————

With the WQDY success to encourage us, Dan Hollingdale—who became my sales manager—suggested that we acquire another station or two and start a tiny network. We bought WMKR in Millinocket and WHOU in Houlton, forming the Pinetree Network, a triangle of three cities about one hundred miles apart in each direction. Although the other stations didn't do as well as WQDY, I sold them and made a handsome profit. About ten years ago, I sold WQDY to Dan Hollingdale. Today, I'm proud to report, it grosses over $600,000 a year, and both Dan and I are extremely happy with our association over the years.

By that time, I'd also sold my liquor store in New York. Some of Governor Nelson Rockefeller's appointees on the State Liquor Authority had been convicted of accepting bribes. Presumably to salvage a certain amount of dignity from a humiliating scenario, the governor removed price control on liquor, enabling big department stores like Macy's and Gimbel's to stock liquor, sell at cost, drive out any number of small independents, and attract consumers into their aisles to buy TVs and sofas in the process. A liquor license had previously been like a cab license—exorbitant, coveted, hard to acquire. Suddenly almost anyone could have a liquor store. Prior to this legislation that killed its value, I could have gotten $300,000 or $400,000 for my shop. By 1967 I considered myself fortunate to be selling it for $25,000 plus inventory. Let's drink a toast to Rockefeller.

With the store out of our hands, Mil and I decided we had no reason to live in New York any longer. We loved our place in Maine in the summer and our Florida lair in the winter, and having three houses is an awful chore. Constant packing and unpacking. Three sets of linen. Mil, who I admit did most of the packing, unpacking, and shopping for three locations, had no objections to reducing ourselves to two. We moved to Florida, making it our permanent address, and planned that for six months each year, we would vacation in Maine.

In Florida and a little restless, I went into the building business with my friend Jack Edwards. We'd buy lots, build on them, and resell very lovely properties. We put up three in Sea Ranch Lakes, one of the most attractive areas in all of Ft. Lauderdale, and maybe in the United States.

One day, in January 1970, I received a telephone call from a young man by the name of Bart Seidler. Bart, a law student at the University of Pennsylvania, had an idea:

"Bob, I promote shows around colleges, and we'd like to have you come to the University of Pennsylvania and do one for us."

"Who's us?"

"Us students."

"What kind of a show?"

"Well, you know. We're all

Howdy Doody fans. A Howdy Doody show."

"You've got to be kidding me." I really thought he was putting me on.

Then he came up with a great line: "No, we want to relive our happy, carefree childhood days."

Nostalgia for the early Fifties had reached full bloom, as the generation who had been kids with Howdy reached young adulthood with its painful pressures and realities. Vietnam. The assassinations of John and Robert Kennedy and of Dr. Martin Luther King, Jr. Race riots. Demonstrations both violent and nonviolent. And I thought, "If they want to remember those wonderful bygone times, I don't blame them a bit. So do I."

I asked, "What do you want me to do?"

"Do you have any films of *The Howdy Doody Show*? Anything that you can bring along?"

"I have a kinescope of the tenth anniversary show. Everybody's in it."

"Great. Bring that and wear your Buffalo Suit. We'll sing songs. I know the kids will want to talk to you, so we'll have a question-and-answer session."

And then I thought some more, because it's not like I'd been asked to go down the block: "Bart, I'd really love to help out, but you're asking a lot."

"We'll pay you."

"I appreciate your wanting to defray my expenses, but you'll never pay

You wouldn't think I missed this. But I did.

me what I think I should be getting."

"How much do you want?"

With everything I've been writing about my business deals through the years, I'm sure you're expecting a staggering figure. But I knew nothing about colleges and their entertainment budgets. I was afraid he had $100 in mind, and I didn't want to embarrass him. On the other hand, I didn't want to charge off on a wild goose chase to Pennsylvania and have to pick up most of the tab myself.

Anticipating rejection, I leveled with him: "I wouldn't do it for less than $1,000."

"Oh, sure. We'll give you at least $1,000, plus a percentage of the gate."

"Then I can't refuse."

"We'll pay your expenses. We'll fly you first class." The only courtesy he didn't extend—and it would have come in handy just then—is that he didn't offer to pick me up off the floor.

Once the nostalgia wave hit, I did many shows. I didn't just get drenched on Laugh-In. I also got clobbered by Ruth Buzzi's handbag. Howdy couldn't bring himself to watch.

I packed my Buffalo Suit and my kinescope and flew up to Philadelphia. Bart met me at the airport. We did the show in the Irvine Auditorium on Valentine's Day, February 14, 1970.

We'd been off the air ten years, and as I waited backstage, I frankly worried. Who remembered Howdy Doody? Who remembered Buffalo Bob Smith? Bart had certainly made it worth my while to make the trip—or was it? How much was it worth, really, to be reminded that the happy, carefree days of the Fifties were as far away as the moon?

When I appeared on Glen Campbell's show, he obliged me by donning Howdy Doody boots, kerchief, freckles, even puppet strings.

7

THE REST OF MY LIFE

*T*en years earlier I'd contemplated the prospects of one heck of a lengthy vacation—that long-overdue rest which could conceivably take me through the rest of my life.

Instead, in the audience of the Irvine Auditorium, I watched the kids watching the Kinescope. They had better memories than the Flub-a-Dub. They remembered every word. I never before realized how campy it looked, from the long 1957 skirts, viewed from the 1970 miniskirt perspective, to the commercials the students had grown up on. When they saw me do the Wonder Bread pitch and the spot for Hostess cupcakes where I pointed to the squiggles on top and the cream filling inside, they laughed so hard the floors shook.

When the kinescope ended, Bart Seidler introduced me. I walked out on stage in my Buffalo Suit—to the biggest standing ovation of my career. I think the audience seated 1,600, and they'd squeezed in 2,300. Twenty-three hundred kids shot to their feet, going wild. I had tears in my eyes. So did they. I couldn't believe it.

The kids couldn't have been more wonderful to me. They wanted to talk, to ask questions. How old am I? What happened to Princess Summerfall Winterspring? How did I get the idea for Howdy Doody? Does Howdy smoke? If he went to college today, would he smoke grass? Someone would question, "Would he?" and I'd say, "Woody? Oh, please, don't refer to Howdy as Woody. We think of him

A jubilant Peanut Gallery—April 1949.

as our own flesh and blood."

With the exception of the last query, I answered the same questions I'd been answering for two decades, but it felt different. The routine had never elated me before. When I took my final bow, thrilled and ecstatic, I thanked my lucky stars that I'd made the trip to Philadelphia; and regretted that it had to be over, never to happen again.

The *Philadelphia Inquirer* and the *Philadelphia Bulletin* were there. They snapped pictures, which resulted in tremendous press. I received wonderful letters from the president of the university and several deans, telling me what fun their families had with me that night.

Within the next few days, Bart advised me of phone calls from students at Temple University and Villanova. Never to happen again? In fact, it happened again and again. I did a show at Temple, another at Villanova, enjoying the same kind of exhilarating reaction and press.

Dancing on air, I returned to Florida, where I played golf at the Coral Ridge Country Club with public relations ace Jack Drury. Jack primarily specialized in major firms, but included some individuals such as Johnny Carson, Ed McMahon, and

Bobby Riggs among his clientele. I mentioned the colleges to him, conversationally. He amazed me by suggesting the feasibility of a tour: "Come over Monday morning. Bring the clippings and letters. Let's put something together." When we met on Monday, he stunned me again by saying "Are you ready to come out of retirement? College tours are big, big business. Jane Fonda and Ralph Nader are very active on the college circuit now." Aware that neither Fonda nor Nader owned a snappy outfit from the Sigafoose tribe, I knew I had something unique to offer.

I told Jack, "You're on."

Jack culled through the material, assembling a most attractive brochure and promotional package. Several hundred of these were mailed to the larger Eastern colleges. Within three months we had at least forty bookings, and proceeded to reach another high-water attendance mark at the University of Miami. The original plan had called for eight hundred seated in the cafeteria for an eight o'clock show. By seven there wasn't even standing room in the cafeteria. They asked me, "Can you move the show outdoors?" I said that if they could project the film footage outdoors, I didn't see why not. By eight we had nearly three thousand people, on a beautiful, balmy night.

Bart and Jack had set me on one of the nicest parts of my career. It just grew and grew and grew, to over five hundred colleges, some as many as

DONNA: A few years ago I heard that NBC might come out with a Saturday morning *Howdy Doody* cartoon show that wouldn't involve you. How did you react?
BOB: I thought it would be the end of all the warm, wonderful, live Doodyville characters, so I wrote to NBC Entertainment president Brandon Tartikoff, hoping he'd sit down with Burt Dubrow and me to weigh the alternatives.

four times. Harvard booked me for a Sunday night show. When it sold out in four hours, we revamped the schedule in order to give two performances—one at six and one at nine.

A call came from Burt Dubrow, whom I hadn't seen since I sold the liquor store and since Burt went off to college. Burt pursued media courses. Before he left for school, he asked for some fatherly advice. I told him that when I started in radio, I did every conceivable job I could find. Whatever the boss wanted done, I did it, whether it was to play the piano, write the tunes, arrange the music, direct the band, improvise the commercials, or conduct the orchestra. I urged Burt to go that route: "Do everything you can. Try to learn every facet of the industry and you'll find your niche. But remember one thing. This industry pays off in one word. Ideas."

Suddenly Burt reappeared with a solid education in media, offering himself as my road manager: "Just pay my expenses. I don't want a salary. My pay-off will be to work with you and to get the experience." I don't know what I would have done without him. He became my road manager and booked a few shows too. From our tour, he graduated to producing a morning talk show in Chicago, to pre-interviewing and other duties as a producer of *The Mike Douglas Show*, and to discovering Sally Jessy Raphael for network television. Today, as Sally's executive producer, he's a powerful force in the TV industry.

I'm very fond of Burt and consider him as one of my best friends. Hardly a week goes by that we're not on the phone together at least two or three times. Sometimes I'm advising him. Sometimes he's advising me. On current matters. Or else just checking in to find out what's new.

When I played the Fillmore East in 1972, Burt introduced me on stage with the line "All right, after eleven years, the man that every little boy idolized and every little girl wanted to marry—a tremendous Fillmore wel-come for Buffalo Bob Smith!" The Fillmore appearance and subsequent publicity spurred a new wave of Howdy Doody merchandise licensing. I did some of my college material for them—for instance, an interpretation of "Chopsticks" in the styles of Ludwig von Beethoven, Richard Wagner, Johann Strauss, Frederic Chopin, Johann Sebastian Bach, "Wolfie" Mozart ("he was one of the gang"), Sergei Rachmaninoff ("big Polish boy, eight-year-old kid, took out girls of fourteen, fifteen . . ."), and Burt Bacharach (this "Chopsticks" bore a remarkable resemblance to "Raindrops Keep Falling on My Head"). I asked how many in the room were veterans of the Peanut Gallery—and counted two hundred hands. They all remembered getting their gas balloons after the program, their loaf of Wonder Bread, their Ovaltine mug, and their tube of Colgate's.

I sang a "message" song for them that reflected the troubled decade of Vietnam, anti-war demonstrations, rioting, assassinations, and widespread disillusionment, feeling very much as I had when Howdy and I performed "Save a Penny" or "Cross the Street With Your Eyes" so many decades earlier. I prefaced by observing "You know, there was a time when I owned you kids. I had you right here in my hand. And some of you Peanuts really thought I was a hero, like the greatest man in the land. But it's funny. Now that you've grown up, well, there's been a complete turn of

HOWDY AND ME

the wheel. Because I think you kids are the greatest, and here's a song that tells how I feel."

Oh, the world's a mess and that's the truth,
And I ain't feeling blue.
'Cause it's my guess this country's youth
Will take us right on through.
Some folks complain, you kids are nuts,
Your lifestyle just won't do.
But I maintain you kids have guts
You'll take us right on through.
You'll take us right on through the muddy waters,
Through the smoke and through the smog.
You'll feed the hungry and raze the ghettos,
Yes, you'll cut right through the fog.
Oh, the light of truth, it shines somewhere.
Not all of us can see it.
But if you kids can lead us there,
Then man, I say, so be it.
Don't blow it, kids, don't blow it, kids,
'Cause now it's up to you.
Put down the phony, slam the sham,
And take us right on through.
You'll take us right on through the bloody jungles,
Past the dying and the dead.
Oh, won't you lead us to that shining hour

I never get too far from the piano. Not when I did the college shows. Not even when I did this early show with Felix Adler and Emmet Kelly, two of the greatest clowns of all time. This was taken in 1948 when we performed for the Radio Executives Luncheon at the Hotel Roosevelt.

When the world has found its head?
Take us through, right on through.
Right on through, right on through.
Yes you'll take us right on through.
Right on!

Along with the songs, piano numbers, questions and answers, and kinescope, I brought them news of the college

THE REST OF MY LIFE

circuit outside New York. First item: Students would ask me whatever happened to those little boys who caused embarrassing moments on *The Howdy Doody Show*—the little boy in the pumpkin episode, and Kenneth, the party pooper. I'd tell them that we kept a Peanut file on some of the outstanding kids in the gallery, and so I knew about the little pumpkin boy—his name is Peter. Peter Dickey was forty-three years old, lived outside East Orange, New Jersey, and was a member of the volunteer fire department. Yeah . . . he's still putting them out.

"Little Kenneth," I'd continue, "he's forty-five. He lives in Chicago. Of course, he would. That's the Windy City. And you'll never believe this— he works for the GAS COMPANY!"

Second news flash: One of the schools thought it might be fun to rope off the first two or three rows in the front of the auditorium and call it the Peanut Gallery. We didn't set it up on stage, because that would have required performing with my back to them, which would have made me uncomfortable and would have been unfair to them. I certainly didn't want to be ignoring them, but neither did I want to be turning to them at the expense of the audience. So front rows were roped off and decorated. The idea caught on, and other schools took it up.

Some schools charged a few dollars more to sit in the Peanut Gallery. Others awarded the seats to winners of an "I Want to Sit in the Peanut Gallery Because" twenty-five-words-or-less contest. I liked this. We got some clever entries:

I want to sit in the Peanut Gallery because I'll try anything that will get me higher than I am right now.

I want to sit in the Peanut Gallery because during this semester I've already been on Bozo and Romper Room.

I want to sit in the Peanut Gallery because it will make my mother proud. She would say, "My daughter didn't make the dean's list, but she did sit in the Peanut Gallery."

I want to sit in the Peanut Gallery because I'm a premed student and I want to find out whether Howdy Doody was circumcised with a pencil sharpener.

I want to sit in the Peanut Gallery because when I was four years old, Buffalo Bob got me hooked on Ovaltine and I can't break the habit.

I want to sit in the Peanut Gallery because I want to get involved in a culturally enlightening group, action involvement, and a task-oriented progressive movement. The Peanut Gallery holds the key to world understanding and peace. Signed J. W. Bell. P.S. I'm married. I need two seats. (He got two tickets even though he evidently didn't know how to count to twenty-five.)

I want to sit in the Peanut Gallery because by watching your show and not an educational one, I am now at Albany State and not at Harvard.

Among my favorites was one from the University of Alabama in Tuscaloosa. With each letter crayoned in a different color, it read:

When I was only ten,
And very young and moody,
My only goal in life,
Was to marry Howdy Doody.
Now being 20 and educated well,
I've changed my life.
I've seen the light.
I now love Clarabell.
Please let there be no dallery.
Just seat me in the gallery.

There was one more memorable than any of the others. Members of the student activities committee of Oberlin Conservatory of Music met me at the airport. They asked if I wanted to check into the hotel. I felt that first we should stop by the auditorium to make sure there were no last-minute snags.

They'd done a magnificent job of decorating the auditorium, with a Peanut Gallery decked out in crêpe paper and balloons. One student, informing me that they'd run the contest, handed me the winning entries.

I said, "Thanks, fine."

The committee said, "Will you read some of the letters on stage?"

"If you want me to, of course."

"I think you ought to read them now."

"Okay." I shuffled through them one by one, finding them fairly funny until the bottom sheet, which made me blush.

"What's the matter?"

"I can't read this?"

"Why not?"

"It's not very clean."

"You've got to read it."

"What if I don't?"

"The winner has already been told that you'll read it and she'll sit in the Peanut Gallery."

"*She?*" I'd heard that college kids had gotten bolder, but for this I was totally unprepared. The winning entry went like this: "I want to sit in the Peanut Gallery because for the past four weeks, all we've been hearing is that Howdy Doody is coming, and I've never seen a puppet come before."

I couldn't help reflecting on the effort network censors had gone to in order to protect the innocence of her generation in the Fifties; of how we had to drop a device as harmless as the Mangle Wurzel for fear of disrupting growing minds. I believe a law of physics covers this. For every action, there's an equal and opposite reaction.

We knew the college shows couldn't last forever, if only because Howdy's generation would soon be graduating from college and having peanuts of their own. But new adventures beckoned. Milt Neil—the extraordinary illustrator and designer of Doodyville for comic books and licensing items (formerly a valued artist at the Walt Disney Studios)—contacted me to perform for a friend in New Jersey. In a mall.

I asked, "Who's gonna be there? Kids? Parents? If it's whole families, I can't do my college show. That's strictly nostalgia, for the college crowd, the alumni."

"Are you refusing me?"

"No, I'm thinking how nice it will be to work with Lew Anderson as Clarabell again."

Milt, Lew, and I went to work on a mall show, with skits, music, ample seltzer, and Milt sketching Doodyville characters. It fascinated people when Milt whipped out a sheet of drawing paper maybe two feet by three feet and, within two minutes, covered it with gorgeous full-color portraits of the Flub-a-Dub, Dilly, Mr. Bluster, and Howdy Doody. We conducted trivia contests, awarding those pictures to the winners.

John Kraus, who manages a string of malls, began booking me frequently. He sees the relationship among Howdy Doody, television, and shopping centers as "unavoidable.

These are about the only industries that a man or woman forty years old could have shared an infancy and grown up with."

From one mall show, we progressed to hundreds. For some, as many as ten thousand children, parents, and grandparents showed up. I loved doing these for three generations of fans. The alumni came, bringing their kids with them, and their parents. The children only knew Howdy from what their moms and dads told them. Nostalgia meant nothing to them. We had to win them over on the strength of our show. I guess some things never change. When they see Clarabell sneaking up on Buffalo Bob with a bottle of seltzer, kids did and doubtless forever will warn me at the tops of their lungs, all the while in gales of more laughter than their little lungs could possibly hold. Grandparents are wonderful, too, thanking me for being their "favorite baby-sitter" and sharing their memories with me. One forty-year-old woman, accompanied by her sixty-year-old mother, confided to me, "I have two sisters and three brothers, and if anyone came to our home in the Fifties between five thirty and six o'clock, they could tell in a minute if any of us had misbehaved. If anyone sat in the living room

🖙 *Clarabell (Lew Anderson) attempts to expand his already wide range of musical talents. The horn didn't sound any different, but he cleared the wax from my ears.*

faced away from the TV set, that was the naughty kid."

I asked, "How do you mean?"

Answered her mom, "I wouldn't take the show away from them. That would have been too severe. I punished them with 'You can't watch Howdy Doody tonight. You can only listen. You can't watch.' "

All in all, the mall crowd adds up to a terrific audience—the dimples, pimples, and wrinkles.

Between the mall shows and, without any question, the return to television of *The Mickey Mouse Club*, we saw a resurgence of interest in Howdy Doody. Stores clamored for Howdy Doody merchandise—particularly in the malls where Lew, Milt, and I appeared, but truly, all over. With Roger Muir and Jack Drury, I set about getting Howdy back on the air. We'd had what might be termed nibbles, but none of the networks bought it. Jack procured an angel for us, who backed a one-hour pilot, which lead to a syndication sale in 1976. We ran the pilot as a special in each of the syndicated markets. The specials sold the series, providing us with the funds to complete the package. Dr. Jack Weinstock had passed away, so Willie Gilbert wrote the series with Nick Nicholson.

I think we were too ambitious in our grand scheme. To begin with, we got a new Howdy, one with vinyl hair. Almost a mod Howdy. Milt did a great job designing him, and I understand the reasoning. But I felt disloyal to my little pal whose hair was painted on, and I honestly didn't like his successor as much. You get used to seeing something one way for thirteen years. Anyway, I had. To this day when I do autographs and offer people a choice of photos, I show them one of me with the old Howdy and one of me with the new Howdy, and they don't want any part of the new Howdy picture. I have a drawer of them at home. I wish I knew what to do with the stack. Yet we'd listened to dire predictions that the old puppets were hackneyed, weatherbeaten, and age-old. "We can't be fuddy duddies. It's 1976!" We did it, and there's no redoing the past. Hindsight is great. Monday-morning quarterbacking will get you nowhere.

Now we had a new Mr. Bluster, a new Dilly Dally, a new Flub-a-Dub, all of whose mouths were supposed to function electronically. In other words, nobody had to pull their mouth strings to make them speak. Howdy had something built inside his head so that whenever I would talk for him, his mouth would operate in perfect synchronization with my voice.

This was marvelous. This was absolutely a revolution, revolutionary. It was unbelievably great—when it worked. But it didn't work a tenth of the time, and we were constantly fixing puppets. Ultimately, we went back to strings.

We had a Peanut Gallery that, instead of seating 40 kids, sat 250; and no longer were they children only, but children with their parents. We had our puppet bridge and our performance area facing the audience, and sets in limbo like Mr. Bluster's room and the canteen apart from that area, which we could shoot and incorporate into the broadcast footage.

The resulting effort lacked charm and intimacy. I have to feel it was all production—albeit excellent production—but no warmth. The scope of the production squeezed out the warmth. That's the downside. The bright side is that many of the shows were top quality. We did them as weekly serials, with cliffhangers that started on Monday and wrapped up on Friday. We had the music of the Howdy Doody Doodlers—eight marvelous musicians. We had comedy (which included inside jokes that probably amused us more than it tickled the kids).

We taped them from Video City in Miami. I commuted from Maine to Miami in the summer. We'd work a week and take a week or two off, then work another week and vacation again. During the part of the year that I lived in Florida, I hardly had to commute at all. Bill LeCornec came from California to do the show, and enjoyed Florida so much that he took up permanent residence. Nick reprised the role of Mr. Cobb and the voices of Bluster, Flub-a-Dub, and the inspector. He lives in Florida now too.

Marilyn Johnstone, from Boston, played Happy Harmony. Marilyn couldn't have been more delightful to work with. No one came to the studio better prepared than Marilyn, and she did a great job on stage. Milt Neil, as Fletcher the Sketcher, did art on camera, as well as contributing an incredible amount of behind-the-scenes creative genius.

Jim Victory, who handled our sales, succeeded in placing us in every major market in the United States. I wish we'd had control over the *when*, but it was out of our hands. In some markets, we were the highest-rated program on the air in our time slot. Chicago gave us an excellent slot, and we did extremely well there. New York City put us on at 2:00 P.M.—which I don't quite understand for a kids' show—and I think it's realistic to conclude that our miserable numbers reflected the fact that most kids are in school, or at least out playing, at 2:00 P.M. Some stations ran us at 1:00 A.M. There are nights that I still go to bed wondering why—actually, telling myself "If this were 1976, I could stay up another hour or two and watch *The Howdy Doody Show*," a hypothesis that seems as ridiculous now as it did fifteen years ago.

We worked hard on those programs, enjoyed doing them, and were gratified by the high ratings in our better time slots—and by another round of well-received Howdy Doody tie-ins. I'm sure that one day soon these shows will be reedited and shown on either network or cable television—and in sensible time slots. When the series ended after 130 episodes, we simply rechanneled our energies into more personal appearances, more parades, more mall shows. Milt left our mall act only for the lure of academia and has been a college professor ever since. Lew and I pressed on as a twosome, through fabulous times, fouled-up times, and some frightening ones.

During one mall show, Lew disappeared in the middle of a routine. Without warning, he dashed off the stage. He ran from the audience and me, into one of the stores. I hadn't a clue what got into him. He just abandoned me.

In less than a minute, he came back. Out of the side of my mouth, I whispered, "What happened?"

Lew replied, "I forgot my nose."

After two dozen years of working with him as Clarabell, I didn't even notice that he started the show in his regular nose. I'm not sure the audience noticed it either until, by contrast, when he returned.

In all the years we've been doing mall shows, we never had any prob-

> DONNA: Tell me about your recent product endorsements—like Coors Beer, Cherry Pepsi, and Black, Beeman's, and Clove gums.
> BOB: I don't hide behind some fictional character. "Buy this because I say so. Me. Little Bo Peep." Never. If I endorse a product, I do it as me.

The sign reads:

NO ← | YES →
CLARABELL

lems with transportation and never missed a flight. We did once have to do an outdoor show in Maryland in driving rain. We would have canceled, but about a dozen people turned out for the event. They begged us to do it from a covered stage on the side of a trailer truck, while they stood on the ground, in the downpour. We asked if they preferred an abbreviated version. They did not. So we did the whole program, and they stayed.

Although we haven't had any transportation mishaps, I work at discouraging them. To that end, I carry my Buffalo Suit and kinescope aboard planes with me. I won't check them through. Whatever other luggage I check, however much else I have to tote along, the suit and kinnie do not leave me. Lew Anderson must, however, check his baggage—a large foot-locker containing his suit, wig, nose, makeup, many props, and seltzer bottles that we use in the show.

We were to arrive in St. Louis on the first day of a three-day appearance. Lew left from the Westchester airport for Chicago. I left from Bangor, joining up with Lew at Chicago's O'Hare. Together we flew from Chicago to St. Louis on the same aircraft. Adjoining seats. Lew. Me. The Buffalo Suit and kinescope. Lew's clarinet. Oh, and his Hollywood Squares jacket from when he and I did a *Hollywood Squares* stint.

When we got off the plane to collect our luggage, Lew's was nowhere to be found. We told the baggage clerk our sad tale. The luggage contained half the show. The clerk said, "If it's not on the plane, I'll have to look into it."

Hours passed. No luggage. I kept after the airline by phone, getting nowhere fast.

At four o'clock, we had to do our show, luggage or no luggage. Lew sat in the audience. We put his clarinet on top of the piano. I opened the show in the usual fashion, not introducing Lew right away because I never do. Clarabell always makes a surprise entrance. I do two choruses of "It's Howdy Doody Time," one where I help them with the words and the other that they do unassisted. I continue, "Okay, you needed a little help on that. But would you need any help if I sing, 'Oh, who's the funniest clown you know?'" Invariably, the audience roars "Clarabell!" in thundering unison. Then I bang on the piano and say, "Oh ho, you remember! What else do you remember about Clarabell?" People yell, "He squirted you!"

"Yes, he used to squirt me. Come on, we'll sing the song." Normally, we sing two verses of Clarabell's tune, and Lew sneaks up behind me with his seltzer. But in St. Louis, at this moment in the program, I had no choice but to concede "I've got bad news. Clarabell isn't here."

"Awwwww!" Everybody groaned.

I turned around and said, "But that's his clarinet on the piano. This is

With Clarabell (Lew Anderson) and Milton Berle, a.k.a. "Mr. Television" and "Uncle Miltie," on a Milton Berle TV special.

129

evidently something Clarabell just learned in Clowntown. See, Clarabell goes to clown school. Sixty-four years ago, we registered him in clown school in Clowntown, and now I guess he's studying the clarinet. I wonder, is there any one of you who would like to play Clarabell's clarinet?"

Lew, of course, stood up sheepishly, in his golf shirt, slacks, and Hollywood Squares jacket. He walked up on stage.

I said, *"Hollywood Squares.* How interesting. Clarabell and I were on *Hollywood Squares,* and we each have a jacket just like that."

Lew nodded.

I inquired, "What's your name?"

He pretended to rap on a door.

"Door?"

He pantomimed pressing a button.

"Doorbell?"

Lew nodded again.

"Oh, that's nice, Doorbell. And you know Clarabell? You go to school with him in Clowntown? I'm glad to hear it, but I asked if someone would want to come up and play his clarinet. Oh, you can?"

Then Lew went into his regular—which is to say sensational—clarinet routine, starting off playing very badly, which gets lots of laughs, but winding up with a great medley of "Yankee Doodle," "18th Century Drawing Room," "The Clarinet Polka," and a knockout version of "It's Howdy Doody Time" and "The Clar-

abell Song." This is always the highlight of our show.

The parents had either known all along what was happening or figured it out by the time Lew played his horn. I'm not sure if the kids understood. But when the applause died down, I stage-whispered, "This *is* Clarabell!" More applause. The biggest hand of the day.

Fortunately, we had a most understanding audience. Afterward, they came up individually to get their personally autographed pictures, to sympathize, and to tell us how lucky we were that it didn't happen more often.

By 6:00 P.M. the airline located our luggage. I was advised, "Good news. We've traced the problem. Instead of a tag that read STL for St. Louis, the suitcase got an SLC sticker for Salt Lake City. So don't worry. It's on its way to Des Moines. From Des Moines, it goes to St. Louis. You'll have it by nine tonight."

"We have another show in an hour."

"Then we promise your luggage will be waiting for you when you get back to the hotel."

We did our second show as we'd done the first, with Lew stepping out of the audience, playing Clarabell's horn, and turning out to be—surprise!—Clarabell. Again, we had a wonderful, appreciative, sympathetic crowd. When I had a chance to phone Mil about the dismal day, she commiserated, "That's great. Why not do all your shows like that?"

The closest we came to tragedy with a mall show was in Rochester, New York, five years ago. We had programs scheduled for Thursday, Friday, and Saturday. After such an appearance, Lew and I usually go out to dinner with John Kraus. But after this Friday night show, Lew said weakly, "Gee, I'm not going with you guys tonight. Just take me back to my room." We tried to persuade him, but he insisted that he felt too queasy.

Lew was a long time getting changed out of his costume. When he reappeared in his street clothes, he looked awful, ashen, and cold. I asked, "Do you hurt?" Shaking his head, he answered that he didn't hurt, but he was sick.

We drove back to the hotel. Actually, John drove. Lew sat in front. I massaged his neck from behind. By the time we got to his room, he'd broken into a cold sweat. Then came the pains. Truckloads of cement driving across his chest. This script I knew to the letter. I said to John, "There's no sense calling anybody. Is there a good hospital nearby? Lew is having a heart attack."

John rushed us to Strong Memorial Hospital, where an EKG and Q-scan revealed that Lew had definitely suffered damage to his heart. Thank God, a cardiologist arrived almost immediately. He confirmed our unofficial diagnosis. Myocardial infarction.

They got Lew into a room, giving him morphine to ease the pain. We waited and waited. The impact of *The Howdy Doody Show* hit home for about the millionth time in my career as the hospital staff shared with me their sense of responsibility that they held Clarabell's life in their hands. The next morning they did a catheterization to determine the extent of the injury. It turned out he'd need a triple or quadruple bypass, which they couldn't perform; they were booked solid for over a month.

We told Lew. He rallied: "Okay, if I'm going to have surgery, I have a friend in New York who is a cardiovascular surgeon. Maybe it's best if I get to New York and have him do it there."

Agreed. Of course, I still had to do two more mall shows, on Saturday, without Lew. I had to tell the people why Clarabell couldn't come. They'd read the papers and heard the TVs and radios, so it wasn't anything they didn't already know. Even so, it tore my heart out to tell them. When I played Clarabell's song, people had their tissues out, wiping their eyes.

*Oh, who's the funniest clown you
    know?*
Clarabell!
*And who's the clown on Howdy's
    show?*
Clarabell!
*His feet are big, his tummy's
    stout,*

*But we would never do without
Clara-Clara-Clara-Bell!*

It was not only hard to do physically—
with a knot in my stomach—but coun-
terproductive to work without Lew. I
depend on his talent so much. And I
realized I might never stand on stage
with him again.

After the show, I autographed
pictures and posed for photos, as Lew
and I always do. People were tremendously sympathetic, offering their
prayers and love.

Planning to stay in the hospital
until he recovered well enough to
travel, Lew sent me home. Several
members of his family remained with
him. My phone rang the next day: Lew
had had another bad myocardial infarction. The hospital couldn't wait. At
ten o'clock that evening, they did
emergency bypass surgery. We're all
extremely grateful to them for the
way they handled it. I can't express
the depth of my appreciation to the
number of grand, caring people at
Strong Memorial Hospital and in the
Rochester area who made us aware of
their concern. Lew received hundreds
of cards and good wishes from our
many fans. I can't think of too many
times I've experienced this kind of
closeness. I'm sure it helped. Lew
pulled through.

We're both senior citizens now;
both survived heart attacks; both
meeting people every week who over-
whelm us with their friendliness, loyalty, and affection; performing
together as Buffalo Bob and Clarabell.
As I've done for the past four decades,
I close the show the way we closed
over 2500 *Howdy Doody Shows*, when
I'd sing:

> *It's time to say goodbye, goodbye*
> *Till our next showtime,*
> *When we'll all be with you again.*
> SPOKEN: *So be with us next time,*
>   *when we all sing:*
> *It's Howdy Doody time.*
> *It's Howdy Doody time.*
> *Bob Smith and Howdy, too.*
> *Say, "Howdy-Do" to you.*
> *Let's give a rousing cheer*
> *'Cause Howdy Doody's here.*
> *It's time to start the show.*
> *So kids, let's go!"*

Arrangement © Edward G. Kean and
Robert E. Smith, 1987

I couldn't think of a better way to
spend the rest of my life.

8

THANK GOD FOR GOOD FRIENDS AND FAMILY

*T*oday, the alumni are middle-aged, and many of our nation's top CEOs watched Howdy and me not only throughout their childhoods, but also caught one or more of my college shows in the Seventies. Happily, I'm still invited to entertain them. Serendipity Enterprises of Pittsburgh books celebrities such as Sid Caesar and Phyllis Diller for corporate speaking engagements. Now they're booking me too, and it's unbelievably great fun to be meeting with my alumni again. I guess it's worth being my age to be able to see how far they've come, and the mark they've made on the world.

There's a Howdy Doody Collectors Club, founded in 1978 to put Howdy memorabilia collectors in touch with each other, to keep the show alive and to preserve its history, to foster buying, selling, and trading among members, and to hold convention and picnics when possible. Roger Muir, Scott Brinker, Bob Rippen, and I attended the club's last convention, on May 5th in Philadelphia, where we conducted seminars, held trivia contests, signed autographs, posed for pictures, and had an all-around terrific time. By the way, the club's monthly paper, *The Howdy Doody Times*, is published from 12 Everitts Hill Road, Flemington, New Jersey 08822.

Between the corporations, the clubs, and the mall shows, I'm on the road several days a week. They keep

I'm flanked by Jackie Robinson (left) and Gabby Hayes (right) for the opening of Jackie's clothing store on 125th Street in Harlem in the early Fifties.

me hopping. But it's not all work and no play. As I mentioned before, I've always been inclined to have fun with my friends. I'm just lucky that so many of my friends are, and have always been, the people I work with. When *The Howdy Doody Show* ran, working with these people, or getting to and from the job with them, rarely failed to make my day.

Dayton Allen has this effect on me. When he's through with me, I'm lucky to know what day it is and to remember what planet I'm on. Some years ago, Burt Dubrow had Dayton and me on a local Chicago talk show that he produced. Afterward, Dayton and I waited at the airport together, preparing for departure. He had no luggage. I had a carry-on valise, and I had Howdy in a separate case with me. We walked by a rest room, outside of which the attendant had left her

utility cart. Commandeering it, Dayton tossed my luggage on top of the toilet paper, mops, and rubbish. He then proceeded to wheel it down the corridor announcing "Ladies and gentlemen, this is Buffalo Bob Smith. *Cheap* Buffalo Bob Smith. Very rich man, but very cheap. Won't spend a cent on a skycap. Won't get a porter. No, he makes me do it, me, Dayton Allen. This is Buffalo Bob. A very cheap man!"

Just for that, I didn't tip him.

When I go out in mufti, I'm not recognized. This particularly became true after I found I needed glasses. I wore them in public, but not on the air. In my glasses, without my Buffalo suit, I could go out where people didn't expect to see me and had a good chance of fading into the crowd. During one of the World Series "subway series," Gabby Hayes and I drove down the Merritt Highway to Yankee Stadium to watch a game. We saw a patrol car that, without warning, took off in hot pursuit of us with siren blaring and lights flashing. Gabby told me I must have been speeding. I said I couldn't have been. The police officer motioned me to pull over. I stopped the car and walked to him. Ignoring me, he went up to Gabby in the car: "Mr. Hayes, my son is a fan of yours. May I have your autograph?"

It was nearly impossible not to recognize Gabby. Ordinary people didn't wear beards then, but he had this fat white beard and long hair like a Western prospector. When he spoke—pure Dodge City lingo—who else could he be but Gabby Hayes? When he'd chatted with the officer and signed a few autographs, he asked, "Don't you want my friend's autograph?"

The officer squinted at me like he thought I'd steal his pen: "Why would I want his autograph?"

"Because he's Buffalo Bob."

"*Buffalo Bob!* Ohmigosh!" He handed me his pen and pad. I wondered if it would be worth it to steal them, but not wanting to miss the game, I signed a few pages before driving off with Gabby. We had superb seats at Yankee Stadium, right behind the Yankee dugout. Gabby, unfortunately, didn't get to see twenty pitches. Fans flocked around him, standing in front of him. So far they hadn't noticed me. I said to Gabby, "Do me a favor. Let one of us watch the game. Don't give me away." Then I put on dark glasses and watched the game, giving him play-by-play descriptions of what he missed by doing autographs.

Church, as you may have surmised, is one of my greatest sources

See! I get along with the police force. In this shot, Ptl. Bob Becker, Harry Herman (President of the Police Benevolent Association), and Sgt. Eugene Ahearn salute me in 1950 as "Honorary Chief of Police."

Playing the organ at Carnegie Hall to lead the Lutheran Hour Rally. *With me is the Rev. Oswald C. J. Hoffman,* Lutheran Hour *speaker for 33 years.*

of strength—naturally—but also of friendships and fun. Over the years I've learned that God must have a sense of humor, otherwise I would have been struck by lightning ages ago.

Once the Presbyterian church had the head of the Women's Christian Temperance Union deliver the sermon at the Sunday evening service. As Mil and I were driving to church, I told her I was going to play "How Dry I Am" for an offertory. She made the mistake of turning this into a challenge: "You wouldn't dare." Of course, under the circumstances, I had no choice. I played a very flowery, elaborate version of "How Dry I Am," thinking that if I were questioned, I'd explain it as an artistic arrangement of "Lead Kindly Light," with which it shares the same first four notes. I haven't had any complaints yet.

When we started the Roadside Theater in 1939, my partner Cliff Jones and I needed a bank loan to get the ball rolling. One member of the bank board also served on the board of the Presbyterian church. When he

saw the application, he quickly granted the loan, then had me discharged as church organist because "You will be selling beer on Saturday night, so we can't have you playing in church on Sunday morning." At the end of the summer when our summer theater closed, the church invited me back. I guess I was either washed pure by all the suds, or else the church couldn't find a suitable replacement. The following year the Roadside reopened. This time we had the means to swing it without a loan. My friendly neighborhood banker decided "not to know about it" and kept me on at the church, because the only other available organist had legs too short to reach the pedals.

One Christmas season Hope Lutheran Church in Pompano Beach, where I served as organist and choirmaster, asked me to compose a special arrangement of Christmas songs to be sung by both the adult and junior choirs. I poured my energies into creating an anthem to be proud of, but didn't hear the junior choir sing it until

Stan Musial, Bob Smith, Joe DiMaggio— "the greatest all-star outfield." As the great Detroit Tigers all-star shortstop Alan Trammell was leaving my son Robin's office, he asked, "What do I owe you?" Robin showed him this photo and said, "I'll make a deal. If you can name any two of these players, the visit is free." Trammell replied, "I'm puzzled. I recognize Buffalo Bob. But who are the other two guys?"

a few days prior to Christmas Eve. As I entered the church one afternoon, I heard the children sing it for the first time. Some sang like angels. But three or four tone-deaf youngsters shouted the loudest and sang like Lucy Ricardo. Howlingly. Piercingly. Painfully. I passed among them, listening to each, then confided to our pastor that some of the kids would have to step down. He protested, "You'll break their hearts. They've been looking forward to this for weeks. And one of them—his grandfather is president of the congregation."

I replied, "I wouldn't care if his grandfather were Martin Luther. That kid has got to go."

I didn't want to cause an incident.

More important, I would have hated to hurt any feelings. Luckily, I had an idea. Again I passed among the children while they were singing, asking "Let me see your hands." The ones who couldn't sing, I asked to step aside. Later I said to these monotones, "You kids have such big, strong hands. And you know, this will be a special Christmas Eve children's service, and we're singing during the offertory. Would you—do you think you could—be ushers and take up the collection?" The children jumped for joy at the honor, rocking the balcony with their enthusiasm. The service went off beautifully. Our young ushers were a wonderful addition to the service. To this day, when I rehearse with our

Working out with Phillies' manager Mayo Smith, one of the best friends I ever had. Spring training, Clearwater, Florida, 1955.

church choir and someone sings off-key, at least one person pipes up with "Watch out, or Bob will make you an usher."

On a serious note, I can't over-emphasize the importance of faith in my life. It gave me immeasurable solace through the long illness of my wonderful sister and lifelong soulmate Esther; and when I lost my father, my mother, my brothers, so many friends—and my little grandson Matthew not many years ago.

Matthew, Robin's son, was playing with friends in their backyard in San Diego, which adjoins property that used to be the Camp Elliott tank and artillery testing grounds during World War II. After the rain, metal fragments occasionally wash up. One of Matthew's friends found a ten-inch unexploded shell and began playing with it. Matthew took it away, hiding it in a bush, because he heard that shells could be dangerous. The friend fetched the shell once more and dropped it. It exploded. Robin heard about it on his car radio. By the time Robin got home, Matthew and another little boy had been killed.

Did we ever get over it? How can we? Nobody ever does. But part of life is living with our losses and going on.

I'm proud of Rob, a urologist, his lovely wife, Connie, and his daughter, Kristen. Our number-two son, Ronnie, has a charming wife, Rosemary, a son, Robbie, and a daughter, Meg, both college students. Ronnie is vice president of Morgan Stanley. Our youngest, Chris, has his master's in psychology and is with the Florida State Mental Hospital. His most talented wife, Christine, is a music major, teaches music, plays the church organ, and directs the choir.

They're the joy of my life—children and grandchildren alike. My grandchildren call me "Grampy Buff."

My license plate reads "The Buff." Mil's is "Mrs. Buff." We used to have only one car in Maine, because we only drive one up. That became ridiculous, so we bought a second car to leave in Maine, in order to have two for the months when we live there. I stopped by the Bureau of Motor Vehicles to register it. I know the people there, they're very friendly to me. I asked, "Do you suppose we can get a plate that says 'Howdy' to go with The Buff and Mrs. Buff?"

The gal said, "No problem." She punched it up on her computer. "Oh, sorry, there is a problem. You can't have it."

"I can't have it?"

"No. Elwood Doody from Perham, Maine, has it."

Recognize the guy on the right? It's Spanky McFarland of Our Gang Comedies.

I thought if my name were Elwood, I'd rather be called Howdy too. Howdy too? There's the answer. I said, "I'd like a plate that reads 'Howdy 1,' " which is exactly what she gave us.

And now, at home, there's me and Mil—the love of my life—and Howdy, the little pal of a lifetime. We're the happiest threesome I know.

Really, I didn't do anything to make Bob Hope scowl like that. Maybe his game was off that day. This photo was taken just prior to our doing a show at Ed McMahon's Celebrity Golf tournament, Quad Cities, 1977.

THANK GOD FOR GOOD FRIENDS AND FAMILY ———————

OUR SPONSORS

For an instant trip down memory lane, here's a list of the products that sponsored Howdy and me over the years.

Blue Bonnet Margarine

Campbells Soups and Tomato Juice

Colgate (Dental Cream, Palmolive Soap, Halo Shampoo)

Continental Baking (Wonder Bread, Hostess Twinkies and Cupcakes)

Kelloggs (Rice Krispies, Sugar Frosted Flakes)

Ludens (Cough Drops, 5th Avenue Candy Bars)

Mars Candy Company (Three Musketeers, Snickers, Milky Way)

Mason Mints and Black Crows

Minute Maid Lemonade

Nabisco Honey Wheat Cereal

Poll Parrott Shoes

Royal Gelatin

(Polaroid) Scientific Screen Enlarger

Tootsie Rolls and Tootsie Pops

Unique Toys

Welch's Grape Juice, Grapelade, and Jellies

HOWDY'S CHRONOLOGY

DECEMBER 27, 1947	First performance.
APRIL 1, 1948	Velma Dawson's Howdy Doody debuts.
SEPTEMBER 1, 1948	*American Magazine* endorses Howdy for President.
OCTOBER 1948	Air Force units participate in Operation Howdy Doody.
JANUARY 14, 1949	Howdy Doody inaugurated "President of all the kids in the United States."
MAY 15, 1949	Howdy, Clarabell, and Buffalo Bob participate in "I Am an American Day" in Washington, D.C.
NOVEMBER 1949	Dell publishes the first Howdy Doody comic book.
DECEMBER 1949	Gene "Mr. America" Stanley and Primo Carnera give wrestling lessons to Clarabell.
DECEMBER 1949	Howdy Doody's first record sells 30,000 copies in its first week.
JANUARY 1950	Howdy Doody is granted a fourteen-year U.S. patent, number 156,687, on himself.
DECEMBER 11, 1953	Howdy and Buffalo Bob light the Rockefeller Center Christmas tree for the fourth consecutive year.
JANUARY 1954	Howdy does his shows from Burbank, California.

OCTOBER 1954	Howdy Doody presides over two performances of the Boston Symphony. Clarabell conducts.
JANUARY 6, 1955	*The Howdy Doody Show* reaches the two thousand mark.
MARCH 1955	Howdy is commended for helping collect 300,000 dimes for the March of Dimes.
LABOR DAY, 1955	Howdy initiates NBC's daily color programming.
JANUARY 24, 1956	The Second Annual Doody Dime Day for the March of Dimes.
DECEMBER 28, 1957	Howdy Doody's gala tenth anniversary celebration.
SEPTEMBER 24, 1960	Howdy Doody's last network series show.
AUGUST 1976–JANUARY 1977	One hundred thirty new *Howdy Doody Shows*, taped from Video City, Miami, Florida, are syndicated nationwide.
MARCH 1987	Buffalo Bob and Dr. Jonas Salk are inducted into the Miami Children's Hospital Hall of Fame.
SEPTEMBER 16, 1987	*USA Today* celebrates its fifth anniversary—Howdy and Buffalo Bob are featured guests at a gala in New York City.
NOVEMBER 9–11, 1987	New York's Museum of Broadcasting honors Howdy, Clarabell, and Buffalo Bob. Howdy, Clarabell, and Buffalo Bob perform, and Buffalo Bob and Roger Muir conduct seminars.
THANKSGIVING WEEKEND 1987	Howdy and the gang celebrate Howdy's fortieth anniversary on a two-hour TV special visited by Johnny Carson, Pee-wee Herman, Milton Berle, John Ritter, Jerry Mathers, Dick Clark, and a host of other stars—many of them veterans of the Peanut Gallery. The special is syndicated to more than two hundred stations, reaching 98 percent of the country.
MAY 1989	Buffalo Bob enters the Hall of Fame in Disney World as one of the Ten Outstanding Legends of Televison.